John Trumbull

**M'Fingal**

A Modern Epic Poem in Four Cantos. Fifth Edition

John Trumbull

**M'Fingal**
*A Modern Epic Poem in Four Cantos. Fifth Edition*

ISBN/EAN: 9783744704892

Printed in Europe, USA, Canada, Australia, Japan

Cover: Foto ©Thomas Meinert / pixelio.de

More available books at **www.hansebooks.com**

# M'FINGAL:

## A MODERN

# EPIC POEM,

## IN

## FOUR CANTOS.

## THE FIFTH EDITION,

### WITH EXPLANATORY NOTES.

Ergo non fatis eft rifu diducere rictum
Auditoris: et eft quædam tamen hic quoque virtus,
Eft brevitate opus, ut currat fententia, neu fe
Impediat verbis laffas onerantibus aures.
Et fermone opus eft modo trifti, fæpe jocofo,
Defendente vicem modo Rhetoris, atque Poetæ,
Interdum urbani, parcentis viribus atque
Extenuantis eas confulto.  Ridiculum acri
Fortius et melius magnas plerumque fecat res.
                              Horat. Lib. 1. Sat. 10.

## LONDON:

PRINTED FOR J. S. JORDAN, No. 166, FLEET-STREET.

M, DCC, XCII.

# EDITOR'S PREFACE

## *LONDON EDITION.*

THE Author of this work is John Trum-
bull, Efq. an eminent Counfellor, in
the State of Connecticut, a near relation of
the late Governor Trumbull of that State,
and of Mr. Trumbull the Painter. The
great reputation gained in this kingdom by
the latter gentleman, in addition to that of
Weft, Copley, and fome others of his coun-
trymen, is an honourable teftimony of the
liberal encouragement which of late has been
here given to the arts: an encouragement
which has attracted hither fo many of the

ableft

ableſt artiſts, as well from the new world, as from ſeveral parts of the old.

In the annotations which we have written, to accompany this Edition of M'Fingal, we have confined ourſelves to the ſimple taſk of illuſtrating the alluſions to ſuch circumſtances as appeared to us to be ſo far local and temporary, as to run the riſk of being ill underſtood by the generality of Engliſh Readers. Indeed, ſo cautious have we been to keep within the ſtricteſt limits of our duty, that, on reviewing our work in the printed ſheets, we are apprehenſive of having erred on that ſide; and that many paſſages have eſcaped our notice, which ought to have been explained.

It is out of reſpect to the Reader, that we have denied ourſelves the pleaſure of dwelling on the particular beauties which muſt ſtrike his attention in the courſe of the Poem, or of making any obſervations on ſuch paſſages as require no explanation. Nor ſhall we attempt to give a character of the work

work at large. Our labours in bringing it in this manner before the Public, in a country where nothing fhort of a high degree of poetical merit is fure to reward fuch labours, are a proof, that in our opinion, the work is deferving of their warmeft approbation.

*M'Fingal*, by fome readers, has been called *the American Hudibras;* but, without deviating from the principle laid down above, we may fay that this comparifon feems to have arifen merely from the *meafure* and from the jingle of the double rhymes; but not from the ftyle, manner, defign, or tendency of the work. The ftyle is uniformly far more elevated, and the manner more grave and majeftic, than that of Hudibras,—but not fo filled with thofe perpetual flafhes of wit, which weary our rifible faculties, without gratifying the mind with more durable impreffions. The difference between the two Poems, in this refpect, feems to be precifely that which we feel between the high and the low burlefque. As far as comparifon will go in forming a judgment of M'Fingal, it appears

pears to us, in ftyle and manner, much more
like the Dunciad of Pope, than like any
other Poem in our language. But in the de-
fign and tendency, it differs from the Englifh
Hudibras in a ftill greater degree. The ob-
ject of Butler was, to ridicule republican
principles, and to tickle the nation into good
humour with arbitrary power; and perhaps
we fhall not pay him too great a compliment,
when we attribute in a confiderable degree
to the influence of his writings, that adora-
tion for Church and King, and that fovereign
contempt for every idea of innovation from
the fide of liberty, which have diftinguifhed
the people of England, ever fince the refto-
ration of monarchy under Charles the Second.
We believe the world has not furnifhed an in-
ftance, befides that of 1688, of a revolution,
begun and conducted by the people, without
their putting in any claim to better their con-
dition, or to fecure their rights. They
feemed in that inftance to be of Mr. Burke's
opinion, That they had no rights; and to
be ready to facrifice their lives and fortunes
in fupport of that opinion.

                                        The

The object of Trumbull is directly the re-verse ; it is to ridicule monarchy—to expose the abfurd arguments and fhallow fubterfuges which are uniformly ufed, wherever it is at-tempted to be fupported by reafoning ; and we believe every Reader will join us in this remark, that there is no Poem in any lan-guage where this defign is kept up to fo good effect. Though the ridicule falls in part upon the Englifh nation ; yet we muft obferve that it is upon the nation organifed in fuch a manner, as to render it capable of being dragged into the purfuit of objects which reafon does not approve. It is the *government*, not the *people*, which excites the cenfure of the Poet ; and every honeft man is put into good humour with himfelf, the moment he makes the diftinction. He muft likewife be pleafed with the impartiality of the Author, in aiming the fhafts of fatire at whatever is cenfurable in both parties ; the extravagant zeal of the Whigs, as well as that of the Tories, is expofed without difguife to our difapprobation.

It

It is now fashionable in this country, among moft claffes of men, to condemn the American war, both in its object and its management; but they fay the cruelties which were practifed in it are now paft; and to tell us any more about them, only ferves to keep up a fpirit of mutual averfion between the two nations. If we were precifely of this latter opinion, it might be an argument with us againft bringing forward an Englifh edition of M'Fingal, whatever be the poetical merit of the work.   But we think the opinion ill-founded, if not directly the reverfe of what the fubject would naturally fuggeft. We think, that the more we learn of their fufferings, which the mifguided policy of our government brought upon them, the more worthy we fhall find them of our friendfhip, and ourfelves of theirs; we fhall both unite in a more cordial abhorrence of the principles and the men, who inflict fuch miferies on the human race.   The principle of all offen-five wars is nearly the fame, it is of full-blood kin to the principle of monarchy; and to hold them perpetually up to the fcrutiny of reafon, is greatly to benefit the world; as it tends to haften that period, which we be- lieve is not far diftant, when both thefe prin- ciples will be difcarded.

In this view, we regard the following Poem, not merely as a patriotic work, to be confined to America, but as a work of gene- ral philanthrophy, highly conducive to moral virtue and univerfal peace.

Mr. Trumbull is known in his own coun- try, for many other works of genius and utility, both in profe and verfe. Early in life, while at the univerfity, he publifhed a fatirical Poem, called *The Progrefs of Dullnefs*, in which he expofed, with great pleafantry and effect, the fopperies and follies attendant on the fafhionable modes of education, both in males and females. In poetry, his genius is not confined to the burlefque; he publifh- ed, in the year 1774, *An Elegy on the Times*, a Poem, which deplores with the higheft energy and pathos, the menacing appearance of hoftilities, which then feemed ready to

b 2 burft

burft upon the Colonies from the obftinate folly of fome leading characters in the Mother-country.  In that work he foretold the event of the revolution in America, as a neceffary confequence of our perfifting in the meafures then in agitation.  By a variety of his profe writings after the war, he rendered effential fervice to his country, in preparing the minds of the people for a revifion of their conftitution, and for fettling the prefent fyftem of federal government in the United States.  As a writer of extenfive erudition, and accurate tafte, the Reader, we prefume, will affign him a diftinguifhed rank, from the perufal of the Poem we here offer to the Public; the general eftimation, in which he is held on the other fide of the Atlantic, from the variety and moral tendency of his writings, may be feen in the following character given of him by another American Poet; who, in enumerating the moft diftinguifhed poetical writers of his country, places Mr. Trumbull at the head of the lift.

" With keen-ey'd glance thro' Nature's walks to pierce,
With all the powers and every charm of verfe,

Each.

Each fcience opening in his ample mind,
His fancy glowing and his tafte refin'd,
See Trumbull lead the train. His fkillful hand
Hurls the keen darts of fatire thro' the land ;
Pride, knavery, dullnefs, feel his mortal ftings,
And liftening virtue triumphs while he fings.
Creat Albion's fons, victorious now no more,
In guilt retiring from the wafted fhore,
Strive their curft cruelties to hide in vain,—
The world fhall learn them from his deathlefs ftrain."

*Vifion of Columbus,* Book VII.

In thefe lines there appears to be an allu-
fion to many other writings, as well as to the
work now before us. We are informed that
the character of M'Fingal, his principle hero
in this poem, was never applied to any par-
ticular perfon ; but that he ftands as a repre-
fentative of the Tory faction in general.
The fame is faid of Honorius, the champion
of the Whigs in the Town-meeting.

The *towns* are fmall divifions or diftricts,
into which the State is divided ; in thefe the
people meet for tranfacting public bufinefs,
fuch as choofing reprefentatives to the gene-
ral Affembly, and Committees for various
purpofes.

purpofes.   In thefe meetings, political quef-
tions were difcuffed ; and in thefe originated
the mode of oppofition to thofe Acts of Par-
liament which were deemed oppreffive.

The cuftom of erecting *Liberty-poles*, one
of which furnifhes the fubject of the third
Canto, feems to have been taken from the
*May-poles*, which are found in fome parts of
England.   Thefe are faid to have had a good
effect in the beginning of the troubles in
America ; as the oppofition againft their
being erected and confecrated as an emblem
of Liberty, determined the ftrength of the
Tory party, in every little neighbourhood in
the country.

The *fcene of action*, which the Poet has in
view, muft be fomewhere in the Province of
Maffachufetts ; but we are not able to defig-
nate the particular town.   The *time* is evi-
dently towards the latter end of fummer, in
the year 1775 ; as, by his allufions to mili-
tary operations, it appears to be fubfequent
to the battle of Bunker-Hill, which was in
the

the month of June; and previous to Mont-
gomery's Siege of St. John's, which was
begun in October, of the fame year.

---

THE Notes in this work, which have
been written by the Englifh Editors, are dif-
tinguifhed at the bottom, by *Edit.* Thofe
that are not fo marked, were inferted by the
Author in the firft edition; which was
printed in Connecticut, in the year 1782.

M'FINGAL:

# M'FINGAL:

## CANTO FIRST.

## *The Town-Meeting, A. M.*

W HEN Yankies*, ſkill'd in martial rule,
Firſt put the Britiſh troops to ſchool;
Inſtructed them in warlike trade,
And new manœuvres of parade;
The true war-dance of Yanky-reels,
And *manual exerciſe* of heels;
Made them give up, like ſaints complete,
The arm of fleſh, and truſt the feet,

* *Yankies*, a term formerly of deriſion, but now merely
of diſtinction, given to the people of the four Eaſtern States.
*Edit.*

B                                    And

And work, like Chriftians undiffembling,
Salvation out, by fear and trembling;
Taught Percy fafhionable races,
And modern modes of Chevy-chaces *:
From Bofton, in his beft array,
Great 'Squire, M'Fingal, took his way,
And, grac'd with enfigns of renown,
Steer'd homeward to his native town.

　His high defcent our heralds trace
To † Offian's famed Fingalian race;
For tho' their name fome part may lack,
Old Fingal fpelt it with a Mac;
Which great M'Pherfon, with fubmiffion,
We hope will add, the next edition.

　His fathers flourifh'd in the Highlands
Of Scotia's fog-benighted iflands;
Whence gain'd our 'Squire two gifts by right,
Rebellion and the Second-fight.
Of thefe the firft, in ancient days,
Had gain'd the nobleft palms of praife,

---

* Lord Percy, now Duke of Northumberland, commanded
the party that was firft oppofed by the Americans at Lexing-
ton. This allufion to the family-renown of Chevy-Chace
arofe from the precipitate manner of his Lordfhip's quitting
the field of battle, and returning to Bofton. But the Poet
will tell us the ftory in the courfe of the work. *Edit.*

† See Fingal, an ancient Epic Poem, publifhed as the work
of Offian, a Caledonian Bard, of the third century, by James
M'Pherfon, a Scotch minifterial fcribbler.

　　　　　　　　　　　　　　　　　　　'Gainft

'Gainft Kings ftood forth, and many a crown'd head
With terror of its might confounded ;
Till rofe a King with potent charm
His foes by goodnefs to difarm;
Whom ev'ry Scot and Jacobite
Strait fell in love with—at firft fight ;
Whofe gracious fpeech, with aid of penfions,
Hufh'd down all murmurs of diffenfions,
And, with the found of potent metal,
Brought all their bluft'ring fwarms to fettle ;
Who rain'd his minifterial mannas,
Till loud Sedition fung Hofannas ;
The good Lords-Bifhops and the Kirk
United in the public-work ;
Rebellion from the northern regions,
With Bute and Mansfield fwore allegiance,
And all combin'd to raze as nuifance,
Of church and ftate, the conftitutions ;
Pull down the empire, on whofe ruins
They meant to edify their new ones;
Enflave th' Amer'can wildernefles,
And tear the provinces in pieces.
For thefe our 'Squire, among the valiant'ft,
Employ'd his time and tools and talents ;
And in their caufe, with manly zeal,
Us'd his firft virtue, to rebel ;
And found this new rebellion pleafing
As his old king-deftroying treafon.

Nor lefs avail'd his optic fleight,
And Scottifh gift of fecond-fight.
No ancient fybil, fam'd in rhyme,
Saw deeper in the womb of time;
No block in old Dodona's grove,
Could ever more orac'lar prove.
Nor only faw he all that was,
But much that never came to pafs;
Whereby all Prophets far out-went he,
Tho' former days produc'd a plenty:
For any man with half an eye,
What ftands before him may efpy;
But optics fharp it needs, I ween,
To fee what is not to be feen.
As in the days of ancient fame
Prophets and poets were the fame,
And all the praife that poets gain
Is but for what th' invent and feign:
So gain'd our 'Squire his fame by feeing
Such things as never would have being.
Whence he for oracles was grown
The very * tripod of his town.
Gazettes no fooner rofe a lye in,
But ftrait he fell to prophefying;
Made dreadful flaughter in his courfe,
O'erthrew provincials, foot and horfe;

* The Tripod was a facred three-legged ftool, from which
the ancient priefts uttered their oracles.

Brought

Brought armies o'er, by fudden preffings,
Of Hanoverians, Swifs, and Heffians;
Feafted with blood his Scottifh clan,
And hang'd all rebels, to a man ;
Divided their eftates and pelf,
And took a goodly fhare himfelf *.
All this, with fpirit energetic,
He did by fecond-fight prophetic.

Thus ftor'd with intellectual riches,
Skill'd was our 'Squire in making fpeeches,
Where ftrength of brains united centers
With ftrength of lungs furpaffing Stentor's.
But as fome mufquets fo contrive it,
As oft to mifs the mark they drive at,
And tho' well aim'd at duck or plover,
Bear wide, and kick their owners over:

* As the good Hero of this Poem feems a kind of god-fon
to the Editors, (they having undertaken to make him known
in this foreign country,) they feel themfelves much interefted
in whatever interefts him. It is, therefore, with real concern
that they find this prophecy, like fome of the prayers of Ho-
mer's heroes, but half accomplifhed. The *Hanoverians*, &c.
indeed, went over, and much were they *feafted with blood* ; but
the *hanging of all the Rebels*, and the *dividing of their eftates*,
remain among the unfulfilled parts of his wife predictions.
This, however, cannot be the fault of our Hero, but rather
of our Minifter, who left off the war before the work was
completed. *Edit.*

So

So far'd our 'Squire, whose reas'ning toil
Would often on himself recoil,
And so much injur'd more his side,
The stronger arg'ments he apply'd:
As old war-elephants, dismay'd,
Trode down the troops they came to aid,
And hurt their own side more in battle
Than less and ordinary cattle.
Yet at town-meetings ev'ry chief
Pinn'd faith on great M'Fingal's sleeve,
And, as he motion'd, all by rote
Rais'd sympathetic hands to vote.

   The town, our Hero's scene of action,
Had long been torn by feuds of faction;
And as each party's strength prevails,
It turn'd up diff'rent, heads or tails;
With constant rattl'ing in a trice
Show'd various sides, as oft as dice:
As that fam'd weaver, * wife t' Ulysses,
By night each day's-work pick'd in pieces;
And tho' she stoutly did bestir her,
Its finishing was ne'er the nearer:
So did this town with stedfast zeal
Weave cob-webs for the public weal,
Which when completed, or before,
A second vote in pieces tore.

            * Homer's Odyssey.

                              They

They met, made fpeeches full long-winded,
Refolv'd, protefted, and refcinded;
Addrefies fign'd, then chofe Committees,
To ftop all drinking of Bohea-teas * ;
With winds of doctrine veer'd about,
And turn'd all Whig-Committees out.
Meanwhile our Hero, as their head,
In pomp the tory faction led,
Still following, as the 'Squire fhould pleafe,
Succeffive on, like files of geefe.

　　And now the town was fummon'd, greeting,
To grand parading of town-meeting;
A fhow, that ftrangers might appall,
As Rome's grave fenate did the Gaul.
High o'er the rout, on pulpit-ftairs †,
Like den of thieves in houfe of pray'rs,

---

* Some of our Englifh readers may perhaps remember,
that one of the fubjects of difpute, which brought on the war,
was a tax laid upon tea, on its importation into the Colonies.
We have, therefore, only to inform them, that one of the
weapons of oppofition, made ufe of by the people, was a uni-
verfal agreement, *not to drink any Tea, until the tax fhould be
taken off.* The Committees, here referred to, were called
*Committees of Safety;* part of their bufinefs was to watch over
the execution of the voluntary regulations made by the people
in the feveral towns.      *Edit.*

† In country-towns the town-meeting is generally held in
the Church.      *Edit.*

(That

(That houfe, which loth a rule to break,
Serv'd Heav'n but one day in the week,
Open the reft for all fupplies
Of news and politics and lies,)
Stood forth the conftable, and bore
His ftaff, like Merc'ry's wand of yore,
Wav'd potent round, the peace to keep,
As that laid dead men's fouls to fleep.
Above, and near th' Hermetic ftaff,
The * moderator's upper half,
In grandeur o'er the cufhion bow'd,
Like Sol half-feen behind a cloud.
Beneath ftood voters of all colours,
Whigs, tories, orators, and bawlers,
With ev'ry tongue in either faction,
Prepar'd, like minute-men †, for action;
Where truth and falfhood, wrong and right,
Draw all their legions out to fight;
With equal uproar, fcarcely rave
Oppofing winds in Æolus' cave;
Such dialogues with earneft face,
Held never Balaam with his afs.

* *Moderator* is the name commonly given to the chairman
or fpeaker of the town-meeting. He is here feated in the
pulpit.     *Edit.*

† *Minute-men* were that part of the militia of the country;
who, being drafted and enrolled by themfelves, were prepared
to march at a minute's warning, where-ever the public fafety
required.     *Edit.*

With

With daring zeal and courage bleſt
Honorius firſt the crowd addreſs'd;
When now our 'Squire, returning late,
Arriv'd to aid the grand debate,
With ſtrange four faces ſat him down,
While thus the orator went on:
"—For ages bleſt, thus Britain roſe,
The terror of encircling foes;
Her heroes rul'd the bloody plain;
Her conqu'ring ſtandard aw'd the main;
The diff'rent palms her triumphs grace,
Of arms in war, of arts in peace:
Unharraſs'd by maternal care,
Each riſing province flouriſh'd fair;
Whoſe various wealth with lib'ral hand,
By far o'er-paid the parent-land.
But tho' ſo bright her ſun might ſhine,
'Twas quickly haſting to decline,
With feeble rays, too weak t' aſſuage,
The damps, that chill the eve of age."
" For ſtates, like men, are doom'd as well
Th' infirmities of age to feel;
And from their diff'rent forms of empire,
Are ſeiz'd with ev'ry deep diſtemper.
Some ſtates high fevers have made head in,
Which nought could cure but copious bleeding;
While others have grown dull and dozy,
Or fix'd in helpleſs idiocy;

C	Or

Or turn'd demoniacs to belabour
Each peaceful habitant and neighbour;
Or vex'd with hypocondriac fits,
Have broke their strength and lost their wits."

"Thus now while hoary years prevail,
Good Mother Britain seem'd to fail;
Her back bent, crippled with the weight
Of age and debts and cares of state:
For debts she ow'd, and those so large
As twice her wealth could not discharge;
And now 'twas thought, so high they'd grown,
She'd break, and come upon the town * ;
Her arms, of nations once the dread,
She scarce could lift above her head;
Her deafen'd ears ('twas all their hope)
The final trump perhaps might ope,    .
So long they'd been in stupid mood,
Shut to the hearing of all good;
Grim Death had put her in his scroll,
Down on the execution-roll;
And Gallic crows, as she grew weaker,
Began to whet their beaks to pick her.

---

* *To come upon the town,* in America, does not mean precisely the same thing, as for a lady to come upon the town in London. It is like a poor person in England coming upon the parish, or becoming a public charge. This remark will serve to explain many other allusions to town-regulations in the course of this Poem.    *Edit.*

And

And now, her pow'rs decaying faft,
Her grand climact'ric had fhe paft,
And, juft like all old women elfe,
Fell in the vapours much by fpells.
Strange whimfies on her fancy ftruck,
And gave her brain a difmal fhock;
Her mem'ry fails, her judgment ends;
She quite forgot her neareft friends;
Loft all her former fenfe and knowledge,
And fitted faft for Beth'lem college;
Of all the pow'rs fhe once retain'd,
Conceit and pride alone remain'd.
As Eve, when falling, was fo modeft
To fancy fhe fhould grow a goddefs;
As madmen, ftraw who long have flept on,
Will ftile them, Jupiter or Neptune:
So Britain, 'midft her airs fo flighty,
Now took a whim to be Almighty;
Urg'd on to defp'rate heights of frenzy,
Affirm'd her own Omnipotency *;
Would rather ruin all her race,
Than 'bate Supremacy an ace;
Affum'd all rights divine, as grown
The church's head, like good Pope Joan:

---

* See the act, declaring that the King and Parliament had
" a right to bind the colonies *in all cafes whatfoever.*"
*Edit.*

Swore

Swore all the world fhould bow and fkip
To her almighty Goodyfhip;
Anath'matiz'd each unbeliever,
And vow'd to live and rule for ever.
Her fervants humour'd every whim,
And own'd, at once, her pow'r fupreme,
Her follies pleas'd in all their ftages,
For fake of legacies and wages;
In * *Stephen's Chapel* then in ftate too
Set up her golden calf to pray to,
Proclaim'd its pow'r and right divine,
And call'd for worfhip at its fhrine,
And for poor Heretics to burn us
Bade North prepare his fiery furnace;
Struck bargains with the Romifh churches
Infallibility to purchafe;
Set wide for Popery the door,
Made friends with Babel's fcarlet whore,
Join'd both the matrons firm in clan;
No fifters made a better fpan.
No wonder then, ere this was over,
That fhe fhould make her children fuffer.
She firft, without pretence of reafon,
Claim'd right whate'er we had to feize on;
And with determin'd refolution,
To put her claims in execution,

---

* The Parliament-Houfe is call'd by that name.

Sent

Sent fire and fword, and call'd it, Lenity,
Starv'd us, and chriften'd it, Humanity.
For fhe, her cafe grown defperater,
Miftook the plaineft things in nature;
Had loft all ufe of eyes or wits;
Took flav'ry for the Bill of Rights;
Trembled at Whigs and deem'd them foes,
And ftopp'd at loyalty her nofe;
Stil'd her own children, brats and caitiffs,
And knew us not from th' Indian natives."

" What tho' with fupplicating pray'r
We begg'd our lives and goods fhe'd fpare;
Not vainer vows, with fillier call,
Elijah's prophets rais'd to Baal;
A worfhipp'd ftock of god, or goddefs,
Had better heard and underftood us.
So once Egyptians at the Nile
Ador'd their guardian Crocodile,
Who heard them firft with kindeft ear,
And ate them to reward their pray'r;
And could he talk, as kings can do,
Had made as gracious fpeeches too."

" Thus fpite of pray'rs her fchemes purfuing,
She ftill went on to work our ruin;
Annull'd our charters of releafes,
And tore our title-deeds in pieces;
Then fign'd her warrants of ejection,
And gallows rais'd to ftretch our necks on:

And

And on thefe errands fent in rage,
Her bailiff, and her hangman, Gage *,
And at his heels, like dogs to bait us,
Difpatch'd her *Poffe Comitatus*."
 " No ftate e'er chofe a fitter perfon,
To carry fuch a filly farce on.
As Heathen gods in ancient days
Receiv'd at fecond-hand their praife,
Stood imag'd forth in ftones and flocks,
And deified in barber's blocks ;
So Gage was chofe to reprefent
Th' omnipotence of Parliament.
And as old heroes gain'd, by fhifts,
From gods, as poets tell, their gifts,
Our Gen'ral, as his actions fhow,
Gain'd like affiflance from below,
By Satan grac'd with full fupplies,
From all his magazine of lies.

---

* General Gage, commander in chief of the king's troops
in North-America, was appointed in 1773 governor and vice-
admiral of Maffachufetts, in the room of Hutchinfon, who
had been the moft active agent of the Minifler in fomenting
the difputes which brought on the war.
 The character and conduct of Gage is defcribed with great
juftice in the fubfequent part of this fpeech of Honorius.
                                                    *Edit.*


Yet

Yet could his practice ne'er impart
The wit, to tell a lie with art.
Thofe lies alone are formidable,
Where artful truth is mixt with fable ;
But Gage has bungled oft fo vilely,
No foul would credit lies fo filly ;
Outwent all faith, and ftretch'd beyond
Credulity's extremeft end.
Whence plain it feems, tho' Satan once
O'erlook'd with fcorn each brainlefs dunce,
And blund'ring brutes in Eden fhunning,
Chofe out the ferpent for his cunning ;
Of late he is not half fo nice,
Nor picks afliftants, 'caufe they're wife.
For had he ftood upon perfection,
His prefent friends had loft th' election,
And far'd as hard in this proceeding,
As owls and affes did in Eden."
   " Yet fools are often dang'rous enemies,
As meaneft reptiles are moft venomous ;
Nor e'er could Gage, by craft and prowefs,
Have done a whit more mifchief to us,
Since he began th' unnatural war,
The work his mafters fent him for."
   " And are there in this free-born land
Among ourfelves a venal band,
A daftard race, who long have fold
Their fouls and confciences for gold ;

Who

Who wifh to ftab their country's vitals,
If they might heir furviving titles ;
With joy behold our mifchiefs brewing,
Infult and triumph in our ruin ?
Priefts, who, if Satan fhould fit down,
To make a Bible of his own,
Would gladly, for the fake of mitres,
Turn his infpir'd and facred writers ;
Lawyers, who, fhould he wifh to prove
His title t' his old feat above,
Would, if his caufe he'd give 'em fees in,
Bring writs of *Entry fur diffefin,*
Plead for him boldly at the feffion,
And hope to put him in poffeffion ;
Merchants, who, for his kindly aid,
Would make him partners in their trade,
Hang out their figns in goodly fhow,
Infcrib'd with " *Belzebub and Co.* "
And Judges, who would lift his pages,
For proper liveries and wages ;
And who, as humbly cringe and bow
To all his mortal fervants now.
There are ; and fhame with pointing geftures,
Marks out th' Addreffers and Protefters * :

                                        Whom,

_____

* The *Addreffers* were thofe who addreffed General Gage.
with expreffions of gratitude and attachment, on his arrival
with a fleet and army to fubdue the colonies. The *Protefters*

    I                                        were

Whom, following down the ftream of Fate,
Contempts ineffable await,
And public infamy forlorn,
Dread hate and everlafting fcorn."
  As thus he fpake, our 'Squire M'Fingal
Gave to his partizans a fignal.
Not quicker roll'd the waves to land,
When Mofes wav'd his potent wand,
Nor with more uproar, than the Tories
Set up a gen'ral rout in chorus ;
Laugh'd, hifs'd, hem'd, murmur'd, groan'd, and
Honorius now could fcarce be heard.      [jeer'd,
Our Mufe amid th' increafing roar,
Could not diftinguifh one word more :
Tho' fhe fat by, in firm record
To take in fhort-hand ev'ry word ;
As ancient Mufes wont, to whom
Old Bards for depofitions come ;
Who muft have writ 'em ; for how elfe
Could they each fpeech *verbatim* tell 's ?
And tho' fome readers of romances
Are apt to ftrain their tortur'd fancies,
And doubt, when lovers all alone
Their fad foliloquies do groan,
Grieve many a page with no one near 'em,
And nought but rocks and groves to hear 'em,

were thofe who protefted againft the meafures of the firft Con-
grefs, and the general refolutions of the country.    *Edit.*

        D                                    What

What fprite infernal could have tattled,
And told the autho.s all they prattled;
Whence fome weak minds have made objection.
That what they fcribbled muft be fiction;
'Tis falfe; for while the lovers fpoke,
The Mufe was by, with table-book;
And, left fome blunder might enfue,
Echo ftood clerk, and kept the cue.
And tho' the fpeech ben't worth a groat,
As ufual, 'tifn't the author's fault,
But error merely of the prater,
Who fhould have talk'd to th' purpofe better :
Which full excufe, my critic-brothers,
May help me out, as well as others;
And 'tis defign'd, tho' here it lurk,
To ferve as preface to this work.
So let it be—for now our 'Squire
No longer could contain his ire;
And rifing 'midft applauding Tories,
Thus vented wrath upon Honorius.

Quoth he, " 'Tis wond'rous what ftrange ftuff
Your Whig's-heads are compounded of;
Which force of logic cannot pierce
Nor fyllogiftic *carte & tierce*,
Nor weight of fcripture, or of reafon,
Suffice to make the leaft impreffion.
Not heeding what ye rais'd conteft on,
Ye prate, and beg or fteal the queftion;

And

And when your boafted arguings fail,
Strait leave all reas'ning off, to rail.
Have not our High-Church Clergy made it
Appear from fcriptures, which ye credit,
That *right divine* from heav'n, was lent
To kings, that is, the Parliament,
Their fubjects to opprefs and teaze,
And ferve the Devil when they pleafe?
Did they not write, and pray, and preach,
And torture all the parts of fpeech;
About Rebellion make a pother,
From one end of the land to th' other?
And yet gain'd fewer pros'lyte Whigs,
Than old * St. Anth'ny 'mongft the pigs;
And chang'd not half fo many vicious
As Auftin, when he preach'd to fifhes;
Who throng'd to hear, the legend tells,
Were edified and wagg'd their tails:
But fcarce you'd prove it, if you tried,
That e'er one Whig was edified.
Have ye not heard from † Parfon Walter
Much dire prefage of many a halter?
What warnings had ye of your duty
From our old Rev'rend † Sam. Auchmuty?

---

* The flories of St. Anthony and his pig, and St. Auftin's
preaching to fifhes, are told in the Popifh legends.

† High-Church Clergymen, one at Bofton, one at New-
York.

From Priefts of all degrees and metres,
T' our fag-end-man poor * Parfon Peters?
Have not our Cooper and our Seabury
Sung hymns, like Barak and old Deborah;
Prov'd all intrigues to fet you free,
Rebellion 'gainft *the pow'rs that be ;*
Brought over many a Scripture text
That us'd to wink at rebel fects;
Coax'd wayward ones to favour regents,
Or paraphras'd them to obedience;
Prov'd ev'ry king, ev'n thofe confeft
Horns of th' Apocalyptic beaft,
And fprouting from its noddles feven,
Ordain'd, as bifhops are, by Heaven;
(For reafons fim'lar, as we're told,
That Tophet was ordain'd of old;)
By this lay-ordination valid
Becomes all fanctified and hallow'd,
Takes patent out when Heav'n has fign'd it,
And ftarts up ftrait, the Lord's anointed?
Like extreme unction, that can cleanfe
Each penitent from deadly fins,

* Peters, a Tory-Clergyman in Connecticut, who after
making himfelf deteftable by his inimical conduct, abfcond-
ed from the contempt, rather than the vengeance of his coun-
trymen, and fled to England to make complaints againft that
colony: Cooper, a writer, poet, and fatyrift of the fame
ftamp, Prefident of the college at New-York; Seabury, a
Clergyman of the fame province.

Make

Make them run glib, when oil'd by Prieft,
The heav'nly road, like wheels new greas'd,
Serve them, like fhoeball, for defences
'Gainft wear and tear of confciences :
So king's anointment cleans betimes,
Like fuller's earth, all fpots of crimes ;
For future knav'ries gives commiffions,
Like Papifts finning under licence.
For Heav'n ordain'd the origin,
Divines declare, of pain and fin ;
Prove fuch great good they both have done us,
Kind mercy 'twas they came upon us :
For without pain and fin and folly
Man ne'er were bleft, or wife, or holy ;
And we fhould * thank the Lord, 'tis fo,
As authors grave wrote long ago.
Now Heav'n its iffues never brings
Without the means, and thefe are kings ;
And he, who blames when they announce ills,
Would counteract th' eternal counfels.
As when the Jews, a murm'ring race,
By conftant grumblings, fell from grace,
Heav'n taught them firft to know their diftance
By famine, flav'ry, and Philiftines ;
When thefe could no repentance bring,
In wrath it fent them laft a king :

---

* See the Modern Metaphyfical Divinity.

1                                              So

So nineteen, 'tis believ'd, in twenty
Of modern kings for plagues are sent you;
Nor can your cavillers pretend,
But that they answer well their end.
'Tis yours to yield to their command,
As rods in Providence's hand;
And if it means to send you pain,
You turn your noses up in vain;
Your only way's in peace to bear it,
And make necessity a merit.
Hence sure perdition must await
The man who rises 'gainst the state,
Who meets at once the damning sentence,
Without one loop-hole for repentance;
E'en tho' he gain the royal fee,
And rank among *the pow'rs that be :*
For hell is theirs, the Scripture shows,
Whoe'er *the pow'rs that be* oppose,
And all those pow'rs (I am clear that 'tis so)
Are damn'd for ever, *ex officio.*"

    " Thus far our Clergy; but 'tis true,
We lack'd not earthly reas'ners too.
Had I the * Poet's brazen lungs
As sound-board to his hundred tongues,

---

    * Virgil's Æneid, 6th book, line 625.

I could

I could not half the fcribblers mufter
That fwarm'd round Rivington * in clufter ;
Affemblies, Councilmen, forfooth ;
Brufh, Cooper, Wilkins, Chandler, Booth.
Yet all their arguments and fap'ence,
You did not value at three half-pence.
Did not our Maffachufettenfis †
For your conviction ftrain his fenfes ?
Scrawl ev'ry moment he could fpare,
From cards and barbers and the fair ;
Show, clear as fun in noon-day heavens,
You did not feel a fingle grievance ;
Demonftrate all your oppofition
Sprung from the ‡ eggs of foul fedition ;
Swear he had feen the neft fhe laid in,
And knew how long fhe had been fitting ;
Could tell exact what ftrength of heat is
Requir'd to hatch her out Committees ;

* _Rivington,_ Editor of the Royal Gazette in New York : a paper which anfwered very well to its title, it being filled with thofe impofitions and falfehoods, which are deemed neceffary to the fupport of Royalty, in any country where printing is tolerated. _Edit._

† See a courfe of effays, under the fignature of Maffachu-fettenfis.

‡ " Committees of Correfpondence are the fouleft and moft venomous ferpent, that ever iffued from the eggs of fedition," &c.                          Maffachufettenfis.

What

What shapes they take, and how much longer's
The space before they grow t' a Congress?
New white-wash'd Hutchinson, and varnish'd
Our Gage, who'd got a little tarnish'd ;
Made 'em new masks, in time no doubt,
For Hutchinson's was quite worn out ;
And while he muddled all his head,
You did not heed a word he said.
Did not our grave * Judge Sewall hit
The summit of news-paper wit ?
Fill'd ev'ry leaf of ev'ry paper
Of Mills, and Hicks, and Mother Draper :
Drew proclamations, works of toil,
In true sublime of scare-crow style ;
Wrote farces too, 'gainst Sons of Freedom,
All for your good, and none would read 'em ;
Denounc'd damnation on their frenzy,
Who died in Whig-impenitency ;
Affirm'd that Heav'n would lend us aid,
As all our Tory-writers said;
And calculated so its kindness,
He told the moment when it join'd us."

* Attorney-General of Massachusetts-Bay, a Judge of Ad-
miralty, Gage's chief Advertiser and Proclamation-maker,
author of a farce called the Americans Rouzed, and of a
great variety of essays on the Ministerial side, in the Boston
news-papers.

" 'Twas

" 'Twas then belike, Honorius cried,
When you the public faft defied,
Refus'd to Heav'n to raife a prayer,
Becaufe you'd no connections there :
And fince, with rev'rent hearts and faces,
To Governors you'd made addreffes,
In them who made you Tories, feeing
You liv'd and mov'd and had your being;
Your humble vows you would not breathe
To pow'rs you'd no acquaintance with."

" As for your fafts, replied our 'Squire,
What circumftance could fafts require?
We kept them not, but 'twas no crime;
We held them merely lofs of time.
For what advantage, firm and lafting,
Pray, did you ever get by fafting?
And what the gains that can arife
From vows and off'rings to the fkies?
Will Heav'n reward with pofts and fees,
Or fend us Tea, as Configees *,
Give penfions, fal'ries, places, bribes,
Or chufe us judges, clerks, or fcribes?
Has it commiffions in its gift,
Or cafh, to ferve us at a lift?

---

* Alluding to the famous cargo of tea, which was funk in
Bofton Harbour, the Configees of which were the tools of
General Gage.                                        *Edit.*

E                                  Are

Are acts of parliament there made,
To carry on the placeman's trade?
Or has it pafs'd a fingle bill
To let us plunder whom we will?
And look our lift of place-men all over;
Did Heav'n appoint our chief judge, Oliver,
Fill that high bench with ignoramus;
Or has it councils by mandamus?
Who made that wit of * water-gruel,
A Judge of Admiralty, Sewall?
And were they not mere earthly ftruggles,
That rais'd up Murray, fay, and Ruggles?
Did Heav'n fend down, our pains to med'cine,
That old fimplicity of Edfon;
Or by election pick out from us,
That Marfhfield blund'rer Nat. Ray Thomas:
Or had it any hand in ferving
A Loring, Pepp'rell, Browne, or Erving?"

    " Yet we've fome faints, the very thing,
We'll pit againft the beft you'll bring.
For can the ftrongeft fancy paint
Than Hutchinfon a greater faint?
Was there a parfon us'd to pray
At times more reg'lar twice a day;
As folks exact have dinners got,
Whether they've appetites or not?

        * A proper emblem of his genius.

                                    Was

Was there a zealot more alarming
'Gainſt public vice to hold forth ſermon ;
Or fix'd at church, whoſe inward motion
Roll'd up his eyes with more devotion ?
What Puritan could ever pray
In Godlier tone, than treas'rer * Gray,
Or at town-meetings ſpeechify'ng,
Could utter more melodious whine,
And ſhut his eyes and vent his moan,
Like owl afflicted in the ſun ?
Who, once ſent home his canting rival,
Lord Dartmouth's ſelf, might out-be-drivel."

  " Have you forgot, Honorious cried,
How your prime ſaint the truth defied †,
Affirm'd he never wrote a line
Your charter'd rights to undermine ;
When his own letters then were by,
That prov'd his meſſage all a lie ?
How many promiſes he ſeal'd,
To get th' oppreſſive acts repeal'd ;
Yet, once arriv'd on England's ſhore,
Set on the Premier to paſs more ?
But theſe are no defects, we grant,
In a right loyal Tory ſaint,

---

  * Treaſurer of Maſſachuſetts-Bay, and one of the Manda-
mus Council.

  † The detection of falſehood in Governor Hutchinſon, here
alluded to, is a curious little hiſtory. It is told at large in
*The Remembrancer*, publiſhed by Almon, Vol. I.      *Edit.*

Whofe godlike virtues muſt with eafe
Atone ſuch venal crimes as theſe:
Or ye perhaps in Scripture ſpy
A new commandment, " Thou ſhalt lie;"
And if 't be ſo (as who can tell ?)
There's no one ſure ye keep ſo well."

 " Quoth he, For lies and promiſe breaking
Ye need not be in ſuch a taking;
For lying is, we know and teach,
The higheſt privilege of ſpeech;
The univerſal Magna Charta,
To which all human race is party;
Whence children firſt, as David ſays,
Lay claim to 't in their earlieſt days;
The only ſtratagem in war
Our Gen'rals have occaſion for;
The only freedom of the preſs
Our politicians need in peace:
And 'tis a ſhame you wiſh t' abridge us
Of theſe our darling privileges.
Thank heav'n, your ſhot have miſs'd their aim,
For lying is no ſin, or ſhame."

 " As men laſt wills may change again,
Tho' drawn in name of God, Amen;
Beſure they muſt have much the more,
O'er promiſes as great a pow'r,
Which, made in haſte, with ſmall inſpection,
So much the more will need correction;

       And

And when they've carelefs fpoke, or penn'd 'em,
Have right to look 'em o'er and mend 'em;
Revife their vows, or change the text,
By way of codicil annex'd,
Turn out a promife, that was bafe,
And put a better in its place.
So Gage of late agreed, you know,
To let the Bofton people go;
Yet when he faw 'gainft troops that brav'd him,
They were the only guards that fav'd him,
Kept off that Satan of a Putnam *,
From breaking in to maul and mutt'n him :
He'd too much wit fuch leagues t' obferve,
And fhut them in again to ftarve."
  " So Mofes writes, when female Jews
Made oaths and vows unfit for ufe,
Their parents then might fet them free
From that confc'entious tyranny:
And fhall men feel that fpir'tual bondage
For ever, when they grow beyond age;
Nor have pow'r their own oaths to change?
I think the tale were very ftrange.

* General Putnam of Connecticut, who had gained great reputation as a Partizan officer in the war before laft, came forward with activity in the beginning of the war of independence; but his age and infirmities obliged him foon to quit the field.                                                         *Edit.*

Shall

Shall vows but bind the ftout and ftrong,
And let go women weak and young,
As nets enclofe the larger crew,
And let the fmaller fry creep thro'?
Befides, the Whigs have all been fet on,
The Tories to affright and threaten,
Till Gage, amidft his trembling fits,
Has hardly kept him in his wits;
And tho' he fpeak with art and finefle.
'Tis faid beneath *durefs per minas.*
For we're in peril of our fouls
From feathers, tar and lib'rty-poles :
And vows extorted are not binding
In law, and fo not worth the minding.
For we have in this hurly-burly
Sent off our confciences on furlow;
Thrown our religion o'er in form,
Our fhip to lighten in the ftorm.
Nor need we blufh your Whigs before;
If we've no virtue, you've no more."

     " Yet black with fins, would ftain a mitre,
Rail ye at crimes by ten tints whiter?
And, ftuff'd with choler atrabilious,
Infult us here for peccadilloes?
While all your vices run fo high
That mercy fcarce could find fupply :
While, fhould you offer to repent,
You'd need more fafting days than Lent,

          2

More groans than haunted church-yard vallies,
And more confeſſions than broad-alleys *.
I'll ſhow you all at fitter time,
Th' extent and greatneſs of your crime,
And here demonſtrate to your face,
Your want of virtue, as of grace,
Evinc'd from topics old and recent:
But thus much muſt ſuffice at preſent.
To th' after portion of the day,
I leave what more remains to ſay;
When I've good hope you'll all appear,
More fitted and prepar'd to hear,
And griev'd for all your vile demeanour:
But now 'tis time t' adjourn for dinner."

* Alluding to a ſpecies of church-diſcipline, where a perſon
is obliged to ſtand in an ile of the church, called the *broad-
alley*, name the offence of which he has been guilty, and aſk
pardon of his brethren.     *Edit.*

END OF CANTO FIRST.

# M'FINGAL:

## CANTO SECOND.

## *The Town-Meeting, P. M.*

THE Sun, who never ſtops to dine,
Two hours had paſs'd the mid-way line,
And driving at his uſual rate,
Laſh'd on his downward car of ſtate.
And now expir'd the ſhort vacation,
And dinner done in epic faſhion;
While all the crew beneath the trees,
Eat pocket-pies, or bread and cheeſe;
Nor ſhall we, like old Homer, care
To verſify the bill of fare.
For now each party, feaſted well,
Throng'd in, like ſheep, at ſound of bell,
With equal ſpirit took their places;
And meeting op'd with three Oh yeſſes:

When

When firſt the daring Whigs t' oppoſe,
Again the great M'Fingal roſe,
Strech'd magiſterial arm amain,
And thus aſſum'd th' accuſing ſtrain.

"Ye Whigs attend, and hear, affrighted,
The crimes whereof ye ſtand indicted;
The ſins and folly paſt all compaſs,
That prove you guilty, or *non-compos*.
I leave the verdict to your ſenſes,
And jury of your conſciences;
Which, tho' they're neither good nor true,
Muſt yet convict you and your crew.
Ungrateful ſons! a factious band,
That riſe againſt your parent-land!
Ye viper race, that burſt in ſtrife
The welcome womb that gave you life,
Tear with ſharp fangs and forked tongue,
Th' indulgent bowels, whence you ſprung;
And ſcorn the debt of obligation
You juſtly owe the Britiſh nation,
Which ſince you cannot pay, your crew
Affect to ſwear 'twas never due.

"Did not the deeds of England's Primate *
Firſt drive your fathers to this climate,
Whom jails, and fines, and ev'ry ill
Forc'd to their good againſt their will?

* The perſecutions of the Engliſh Church under Archbiſhop Laud, are well known to have been the cauſe of the peopling of New-England. *Edit.*

F Ye

Ye owe to their obliging temper
The peopling your new-fangled empire,
While ev'ry British act and canon
Stood forth, you *causa sine qua non.*
Did they not send you charters o'er,
And give you lands you own'd before,
Permit you all to spill your blood,
And drive out heathen where you could ;
On these mild terms, that, conquest won,
The realm you gain'd should be their own ?
Or when of late attack'd by those,
Whom her connection made your foes *,
Did they not then, distrest in war,
Send Gen'rals to your help from far,
Whose aid you own'd in terms less haughty,
And thankfully o'erpaid your quota ?
Say, at what period did they grudge
To send you Governor or Judge,
With all their missionary crew †,
To teach you law and gospel too ?

---

* The war of 1755, between the English and the French,
was doubtlefs excited by circumſtances foreign to the intereſts
of thoſe colonies which now form the United States. Thoſe
colonies, however, paid more than their proportion of the ex-
pence, and the balance was repaid by our government after
the war.    *Edit.*

† The *miſſionaries* were clergymen, ordained by the Biſhop
of London, and settled in America. Thoſe in the northern
Colonies were generally attached to the Royal cauſe. *Edit.*

         Brought

Brought o'er all felons in the nation,
To help you on in population ;
Propos'd their Bifhops to furrender,
And made their Priefts a legal tender,
Who only afk'd, in furplice clad,
The fimple tythe of all you had :
And now to keep all knaves in awe,
Have fent their troops t' eftablifh law,
And with gunpowder, fire, and ball,
Reform your people one and all.
Yet, when their infolence and pride
Have anger'd all the world befide,
When fear and want at once invade,
Can you refufe to lend them aid ;
And rather rifque your heads in fight,
Than gratefully throw in your mite ?
Can they for debts make fatisfaction,
Should they difpofe their realm by auction ;
And fell of Britain's goods and land all
To France and Spain by inch of candle ?
Shall good king George, with want oppreft,
Infert his name in bankrupt lift,
And fhut up fhop, like failing merchant,
That fears the bailiffs fhould make fearch in't ;
With poverty fhall princes ftrive,
And nobles lack whereon to live ?
Have they not rack'd their whole inventions,
To feed their brats on pofts and penfions,

F 2

Made

Made ev'n Scotch friends with taxes groan,
And pick'd poor Ireland to the bone ;
Yet have on hand, as well deferving,
Ten thoufand baftards left for ftarving ?
And can you now, with confcience clear,
Refufe them an afylum here,
Or not maintain in manner fitting,
Thefe genuine fons of Mother Britain ?
T' evade thefe crimes of blackeft grain,
You prate of Liberty in vain,
And ftrive to hide your vile defigns,
With terms abftrufe, like fchool-divines.

   " Your boafted patriotifm is fcarce,
And country's love is but a farce :
And after all the proofs you bring,
We Tories know there's no fuch thing ;
Our Englifh writers of great fame
Prove public virtue but a name.
Hath not * Dalrymple fhow'd in print,
And * Johnfon too, there's nothing in't ?
Produc'd you demonftration ample,
From other's and their own example,
That felf is ftill, in either faction,
The only principle of action ;
The loadftone, whofe attracting tether
Keeps the politic world together :
And, 'fpite of all your double-dealing,
We Tories know 'tis fo, by feeling.

          * Minifterial Penfioners.

                              " Who

" Who heeds your babbling of tranfmitting
Freedom to brats of your begetting,
Or will proceed as though there were a tie,
Or obligation to pofterity?
We get 'em, bear 'em, breed and nurfe;
What has poft'rity done for us,
That we, left they their rights fhould lofe,
Should truft our necks to gripe of noofe?

" And who believes you will not run?
You're cowards, ev'ry mother's fon;
And fhould you offer to deny,
We've witneffes to prove it by.
Attend th' opinion firft, as referee,
Of your old Gen'ral, ftout Sir Jeffery *,
Who fwore that with five thoufand foot
He'd rout you all, and, in purfuit,
Run thro' the land as eafily,
As camel thro' a needle's eye.
Did not the valiant Col'nel Grant
Againft your courage make his flant,
Affirm your univerfal failure
In ev'ry principle of valour,
And fwear no fcamp'rers e'er could match you,
So fwift, a bullet fcarce could catch you?
And will ye not confefs in this,
A judge moft competent he is,
Well fkill'd on runnings to decide,
As what himfelf has often tried?

* Sir Jeffery, now Lord Amherft.　　　　*Edit.*

'Twould

'Twould not, methinks, be labour loft,
If you'd fit down and count the coft;
And ere you call your Yankies out,
Firft think what work you've fet about.
Have ye not rouz'd, his force to try on,
That grim old beaft, the Britifh lion?
And know you not that at a fup
He's large enough to eat you up?
Have you furvey'd his jaws beneath,
Drawn inventories of his teeth,
Or have you weigh'd in even balance
His ftrength and magnitude of talons?
His roar would turn your boafts to fear,
As cafily as four fmall-beer,
And make your feet from dreadful fray,
By native inftinct, run away.
Britain, depend on't, will take on her
T' affert her dignity and honor,
And ere fhe'd lofe your fhare of pelf,
Deftroy your country and herfelf.
For has not North declar'd they fight
To gain fubftantial rev'nue by't,
Denied he'd ever deign to treat,
'Till on your knees, and at his feet?
And feel you not a trifling ague,
From Van's *Delenda eft Carthago* *?

---

* Alluding, as the Editors fuppofe, to a fpeech in the
Britifh Parliament, in which *delenda eft Carthago* was applied
to America. *Edit.*

For

For this, now Britain has come to't,
Think you fhe has not means to do't?
Has fhe not fet to work all engines
To fpirit up the native Indians,
Send on your backs a favage band,
With each a hatchet in his hand,
T' amufe themfelves with fcalping knives,
And butcher children and your wives;
That fhe may boaft again with vanity,
Her Englifh national humanity?
(For now in its primæval fenfe,
This term, *human'ty*, comprehends
All things of which, on this fide hell,
The *human mind* is capable;
And thus 'tis well, by writers fage,
Applied to Britain and to Gage.)
And on this work to raife allies,
She fent her duplicate of Guys,
To drive, at diff'rent parts at once, on
Her ftout Guy Carleton and Guy Johnfon;
To each of whom, to fend again ye
Old Guy of Warwick were a ninny;
Tho' the dun cow he fell'd in war,
Thefe kill-cows are his betters far.

    " And has fhe not affay'd her notes,
To rouze your flaves to cut your throats,
Sent o'er ambaffadors with guineas,
To bribe your blacks in Carolinas?

And has not **Gage**, her miſſionary,
Turn'd many an Afric ſlave t' a Tory,
And made th' Amer'can biſhop's ſee grow,
By many a new-converted Negro?
As friends to gov'rnment did not he
Their ſlaves at Boſton late ſet free ;
Enliſt them all in black parade,
Set off with regimental red?
And were they not accounted then
Among his very braveſt men?
And when ſuch means ſhe ſtoops to take,
Think you ſhe is not wide awake?
As Eliphaz' good man in Job
Own'd num'rous allies thro' the globe ;
Had brought the * ſtones along the ſtreet
To ratify a cov'nant meet,
And every beaſt from lice to lions,
To join in leagues of ſtrict alliance :
Has ſhe not cring'd, in ſpite of pride.
For like aſſiſtance far and wide?
Was there a creature ſo deſpis'd,
Its aid ſhe has not ſought and priz'd?
Till all this formidable league roſe
Of Indians, Britiſh troops, and Negroes,

* The ſtones, and all the elements with thee
   Shall ratify a ſtrict confed'racy ;
   Wild beaſts their ſavage temper ſhall forget,
   And for a firm alliance with thee treat : &c.
                    *Blackmore's Paraphraſe of Job.*

                                        And

And can you break thefe triple bands
By all your workmanfhip of hands?"
    " Sir, quoth Honorius, we prefume
You guefs from paft feats, what's to come,
And from the mighty deeds of Gage,
Foretell how fierce the war he'll wage.
You, doubtlefs, recollected here
The annals of his firft great year :
While wearying out the Tories' patience,
He fpent his breath in proclamations ;
While all his mighty noife and vapour
Was us'd in wrangling upon paper ;
And boafted military fits
Clos'd in the ftraining of his wits ;
While troops in Bofton commons plac'd
Laid nought but quires of paper wafte ;
While ftrokes alternate ftunn'd the nation,
Proteft, addrefs, and proclamation ;
And fpeech met fpeech, fib clafh'd with fib,
And Gage ftill anfwer'd, fquib for fquib.
    " Tho' this not all his time was loft on,
He fortified the town of Bofton ;
Built breaft-works that might lend affiftance
To keep the patriots at a diftance ;
(For howfoe'er the rogues might fcoff,
He lik'd them beft the fartheft off ;)
Of mighty ufe and help to aid
His courage, when he felt afraid ;

And.

And whence right off in manful ſtation,
He'd boldly pop his proclamation.
Our hearts muſt in our boſoms freeze
At ſuch heroic deeds as theſe.''
   " Vain, quoth the 'Squire, you'll find to ſneer
At Gage's firſt triumphant year;
For Providence, diſpos'd to teaze us,
Can uſe what inſtruments it pleaſes.
To pay a tax at Peter's wiſh,
His chief caſhier was once a Fiſh;
An Aſs, in Balaam's ſad diſaſter,
Turn'd orator, and ſav'd his maſter;
A Gooſe plac'd ſentry on his ſtation
Preſerv'd old Rome from deſolation;
An Engliſh Biſhop's * Cur of late
Diſclos'd rebellions 'gainſt the State;
So Frogs croak'd Pharaoh to repentance,
And Lice revers'd the threat'ning ſentence:
And Heav'n can ruin you at pleaſure,
By our ſcorn'd Gage, as well as Cæſar.
Yet did our hero in theſe days
Pick up ſome laurel-wreaths of praiſe.
And as the ſtatuary of Seville
Made his crackt ſaint an exc'llent devil;
So tho' our war few triumphs brings,
We gain'd great fame in other things.

      * See Biſhop Atterbury's trial.

                       Did

Did not our troops ſhow much diſcerning,
And ſkill your various arts in learning?
Outwent they not each native Noodle
By far, in playing Yanky-Doodle * ;
Which, as 'twas your New-England tune,
'Twas marvellous they took ſo ſoon?
And ere the year was fully thro',
Did not they learn to foot it too;
And ſuch a dance as ne'er was known,
For twenty miles on end led down †?
Was there a Yanky trick you knew,
They did not play as well as you?
Did they not lay their heads together,
And gain your art to tar and feather,
When Col'nel Neſbitt thro' the town
In triumph bore the country-clown?
Oh, what a glorious work to ſing
The vet'ran troops of Britain's king.

---

* *Yanky-Doodle*, as M'Fingal here relates, was a native Air
of New-England, and was often played in deriſion by the Bri-
tiſh troops, particularly on their march to Lexington. Af-
terwards the captive army of Burgoyne was obliged to march
to this tune in the ceremony of piling their arms at Saratoga.
In the courſe of the war it became a favorite Air of Liberty,
like the preſent *ça ira* of France. It is remarkable that after
the taking of the Baſtille, and before the introduction of *ça ira*,
the Paris guards played *Yanky-doodle*. *Edit.*

† This is Lord Percy's modern Chevy-chace; in which his
lordſhip and his army were chaſed from Concord to Boſton. *Edit.*

Advent'ring

Advent'ring for th' heroic laurel,
With bag of feathers and tar-barrel!
To paint the cart where culprits ride,
And Nesbitt marching at its side *,
Great executioner and proud,
Like hangman high on Holborn road;
And o'er the bright triumphal car
The waving ensigns of the war!
As when a triumph Rome decreed,
For great Calig'la's valiant deed,
Who had subdu'd the British seas,
By gath'ring cockles from their base;
In pompous car the conqu'ror bore
His captiv'd scallops from the shore,
Ovations gain'd his crabs for fetching,
And mighty feats of oyster-catching:
O'er Yankies thus the war begun,
They tarr'd and triumph'd over one;
And fought and boasted thro' the season,
With might as great, and equal reason

                                    Yet

---

* The action here celebrated, confidered as one of the pro-
vocatives to the glorious war which followed, is too important
to be omitted in our explanatory labours.   Yet, by compressing
our narrative into a size convenient for a note, we fear that
we shall fail of doing sufficient honour to this immortal hero
of the feather-bag; whose fame ought to be as dear to us, as
to the Poet himself.   In the winter of 1774 and 1775, our
army at Boston had been stimulated, by their Officers and
                                                       the

" Yet thus, tho' fkill'd in vict'ry toils,
They boaft, not unexpert, in wiles.
For gain'd they not an equal fame in
The arts of fecrecy and fcheming;
In ftratagems fhow'd mighty force,
And moderniz'd the Trojan horfe,
Play'd o'er again thofe tricks Ulyffean,
In their fam'd Salem-expedition?

For

the Tories, to an ardent defire of feeing hoftilities commence.
But thefe inftigators always wifhed to have the Americans *be-*
*gin,* that they might appear to the Englifh nation and to the
world, as the aggreffors; and, from the time of Prefton's
affair in the year 1770, every method of promoting private
broils between the inhabitants and the military had been pur-
fued, without the defired effect.

In the beginning of 1775, as the King's ftandard was to be
erected on the firft of May at Worcefter, fifty miles from
Bofton, the troops feared that they fhould be obliged to
march from Bofton, without having the opportunity of in-
dulging the vengeance which they had promifed themfelves in
that town. To bring forward an occafion for a more ferious
quarrel than had hitherto taken place between the people and
the army, Lieutenant Colonel Nefbitt, of the 47th regiment, laid
the following plan.—The country people being in the habit of
purchafing arms, he directed a foldier to fell to fome one of
them an old rufty mufquet. The foldier foon found a purchafer,
a man who brought vegetables to market, who paid him three
dollars for the mufquet. Though this bargain might have
the appearance of a crime in the foldier (fuppofing the muf-
quet to have been his own, and neceffary to his duty) it never

could

For as that horfe, the Poets tell ye,
Bore Grecian armies in his belly;
Till, their full reck'ning run, with joy
Their Sinon midwif'd them in Troy;
So in one fhip was Leffie bold
Cramm'd with three hundred men in hold,
Equipp'd for enterprize and fail,
Like Jonas ftow'd in womb of whale.
To Marblehead in depth of night,
The cautious veffel wing'd her flight.

could be fo in the market-man, in a country where every human creature had an equal right to carry arms.  But fcarcely had the man parted from the foldier, when he was feized by Nefbitt, and conveyed to the guard-houfe, on Green's Wharf, about the middle of the town ; where he was confined all night.  Early the next morning, they ftripped him entirely naked, covered him with warm tar, and then with feathers, placed him on a cart, conducted him to the north end of the town, then back to the fouth end, as far as Liberty-Tree ; where the people began to collect in vaft numbers, and the military, fearing for their own fafety, difmiffed the man, and made a retreat to the barracks.

The party confifted of about thirty grenadiers of the 47th regiment, with fixed bayonets, 20 drums and fifes, playing the rogues's march, headed by Nefbitt with a drawn fword.

The magiftrates of the town waited on General Gage with a complaint of this outrage.  He pretended difapprobation ; but took no fteps to cenfure the conduct of Nefbitt, or to do juftice to the man who had fuffered the violence.

*Edit.*

And

And now the fabbath's filent day
Call'd all your Yankies off to pray;
Remov'd each prying jealous neighbour,
The fcheme and veffel fell in labour;
Forth from its hollow womb pour'd haft'ly
The Myrmidons of Col'nel Leflie:
Not thicker o'er the blacken'd ftrand
The * frogs' detachment rufh'd to land,
Equipp'd by onfet or furprize
To ftorm th' entrenchment of the mice.
Thro' Salem ftrait without delay,
The bold battalion took its way,
March'd o'er a bridge in open fight
Of fev'ral Yankies arm'd for fight,
Then without lofs of time, or men
Veer'd round for Bofton back again;
And found fo well their projects thrive,
That ev'ry foul got home alive.

   " Thus Gage's arms did fortune blefs
With triumph, fafety, and fuccefs:
But mercy is, without difpute,
His firft and darling attribute;
So great, it far outwent and conquer'd
His military fkill at Concord.
There when the war he chofe to wage
Shone the benevolence of Gage;

* See Homer's Battle of the Frogs and Mice.

Sent

Sent troops to that ill-omen'd place
On errands mere of fpecial grace,
And all the work he chofe them for
Was to * *prevent* a civil war :
And for that purpofe he projected
The only certain way t' effect it,
To take your powder, ftores, and arms,
And all your means of doing harms :
As prudent folks take **knives** away,
Left children cut themfelves at play.
And yet, tho' this was all his fcheme,
This war you ftill will charge on him ;
And tho' he oft has fwore, and faid it,
Stick clofe to facts, and give no credit.
Think you, he wifh'd you'd brave and beard him ?
Why, 'twas the very thing that fear'd him.
He'd rather you fhould all have run,
Than ftay'd to fire a fingle gun.
And for the civil war you lament,
Faith, you yourfelves muft take the blame in't ;
For had you then, as he intended,
Giv'n up your arms, it muft have ended.
Since that's no war, each mortal knows,
Where one fide only gives the blows,
And th' other bears 'em ; on reflection
The moft you'll call it, is correction.

* See Gage's anfwer to Governor Trumbull.

Nor

Nor could the conteft have gone higher,
If you had ne'er return'd the fire;
But when you fhot, and not before,
It then commenc'd a civil war.
Elfe Gage, to end this controverfy,
Had but corrected you in mercy:
Whom mother Britain, old and wife,
Sent o'er, the Col'nies to chaftife;
Command obedience on their peril
Of minifterial whip and ferule;
And fince they ne'er muft come of age,
Govern'd and tutor'd them by Gage.
Still more, that this was all their errand,
The army's conduct makes apparent.
What tho' at Lexington you can fay
They kill'd a few they did not fancy,
At Concord, then, with manful popping,
Difcharg'd a round, the ball to open?
Yet when they faw your rebel-rout
Determin'd ftill to hold it out;
Did they not fhow their love to peace,
And wifh, that difcord ftrait may ceafe,
Demonftrate, and by proofs uncommon,
Ther orders were to injure no man?
For did not ev'ry Reg'lar run *
As foon as e'er you fir'd a gun:

Take

---

* In the ancient wars in America, the term *Regular* was

H                                                applied

Take the firſt ſhot you ſent them greeting,
As meant their ſignal for retreating;
And, fearful if they ſtaid for ſport,
You might by accident be hurt,
Convey themſelves with ſpeed away
Full twenty miles in half a day;
Race till their legs were grown ſo weary,
They'd ſcarce ſuffice their weight to carry?
Whence Gage extols, from gen'ral hearſy,
The great * activ'ty of Lord Percy;
Whoſe brave example led them on,
And ſpirited the troops to run;
And now may boaſt at royal levees
A Yanky-chace worth forty Chevys.
Yet you, as vile as they were kind,
Purſu'd, like tygers, ſtill behind,
Fir'd on them at your will, and ſhut
The town, as tho' you'd ſtarve them out;
And with † parade prepoſt'rous hedg'd
Affect to hold them there beſieg'd;

applied to Britiſh troops, to diſtinguiſh them from the Pro-
vincials, or new levies of the country. At the commencement
of the late war, the ſame terms of diſtinction were uſed. *Edit.*

  * " Too much praiſe cannot be given to Lord Percy for
his remarkable activity through the whole day."

            *Gage's Account of the Lexington Battle.*

  † " And with a prepoſterous parade of military arrangement
they affect to hold the army beſieged."

              *Gage's laſt grand Proclamation.*

                        (Tho'

(Tho' Gage, whom proclamations call
Your Gov'nor and Vice-Admiral,
Whofe pow'r gubernatorial-ftill
Extends as far as Bunker's hill;
Whofe admiralty reaches clever,
Near half a mile up Myftic river,
Whofe naval force commands the feas,
Can run away whene'er he pleafe,)
Scar'd Troops of Tories into town,
And burnt their hay and houfes down,
And menac'd Gage, unlefs he'd flee,
To drive him headlong to the fea;
As once, to faithlefs Jews a fign,
The de'el turn'd hog-reeve, did the fwine.

   " But now your triumphs all are o'er;
For fee from Britain's angry fhore
With mighty hofts of valour join
Her Howe, her Clinton, and Burgoyne.
As comets thro' the affrighted fkies
Pour baleful ruin, as they rife;
As Ætna with infernal roar
In conflagration fweeps the fhore;
Or as * Abijah White, when fent
Our Marfhfield friends to reprefent;

---

* He was a reprefentative of Marfhfield, and employed to
carry their famous town-refolves to Bofton. He armed him-
felf in as ridiculous military array, as another Hudibras, pre-
tending he was afraid he fhould be robbed of them.

         Himfelf

Himfelf while dread array involves,
Commiffions, piftols, fwords, refolves,
In awful pomp defcending down,
Bore terror on the factious town :
Not with lefs glory and affright,
Parade thefe Gen'rals forth to fight.
No more each Reg'lar * Col'nel runs
From whizzing beetles, as air-guns,
Thinks horn-bugs bullets, or thro' fears
Mufkitoes takes for mufketeers ;
Nor 'fcapes, as tho' you gain'd allies
From Belzebub's whole hoft of flies.
No bug their warlike heart appalls ;
They better know the found of balls.
I hear the din of battle bray,
The trump of horror marks its way.
I fee after the fack of cities,
The gallows ftrung with Whig-committees ;

---

* This was a fact.  Some Britifh officers, foon after Gage's
arrival in Bofton, walking on Beacon-Hill after funfet, were
affrighted by noifes in the air (fuppofed to be the flying of bugs
and beetles) which they took to be the found of bullets, and
left the hill with great precipitation : Concerning which they
wrote terrible accounts to England of their being fhot at with
air-guns, as appears by one or two letters, extracts from
which were publifhed in the Englifh papers.

Your

Your Moderators tric'd, like vermin,
And gate-pofts * grac'd with heads of Chairmen;
Your Gen'rals for wave-offerings hanging,
And ladders throng'd with Priefts haranguing.
What pill'ries glad the Tories' eyes
With patriot-ears for facrifice!
What whipping-pofts your chofen race
Admit fucceffive in embrace,
While each bears off his crimes, alack!
Like Bunyan's pilgrim, on his back!
Where then, when Tories fcarce get clear,
Shall Whigs and Congreffes appear?
What rocks and mountains fhall you call
To wrap you over with their fall,
And fave your heads in thefe fad weathers,
From fire and fword, and tar and feathers!
For lo, with Britifh troops tar-bright,
Again our Nefbitt heaves in fight!
He comes, he comes, your lines to ftorm,
And rigg your troops in uniform!
To meet fuch heroes, will ye brag,
With fury arm'd, and feather-bag;

---

* The Author, though a rebel and a foreigner, cannot avoid
this indirect tribute of praife to his ancient Mother-country.
He evidently alludes here to the heads of the chiefs of the
laft Scotifh rebellion, which were fixed on Temple-Bar, and
ferved for fo many years, both as an ornament to this our good
city of London, and as an emblem of our national huma-
nity.                                                    *Edit.*

I                                              Who

Who wield their miffile pitch and tar,
With engines new in Britifh war?

" Lo, where our mighty navy brings
Deftruction on her canvas wings,
While thro' the deeps her potent thunder
Shall found th' alarm to rob and plunder!
As Phœbus firft, fo Homer fpeaks,
When he march'd out t' attack the Greeks,
'Gainft mules fent forth his arrows fatal,
And flew th' auxiliaries, their cattle;
So where our fhips fhall ftretch the keel,
What conquer'd oxen fhall they fteal!
What heroes rifing from the deep
Invade your marfhall'd hofts of fheep!
Difperfe whole troops of horfe, and preffing
Make cows furrender at difcretion;
Attack your hens, like Alexanders,
And reg'ments rout of geefe and ganders;
Or where united arms combine
Lead captive many a herd of fwine!
Then rufh in dreadful fury down
To fire on ev'ry fea-port town;
Difplay their glory and their wits,
Fright unarm'd children into fits,
And ftoutly from th' unequal fray,
Make many a woman run away!
And can ye doubt whene'er we pleafe
Our chiefs fhall boaft fuch deeds as thefe?

                                    Have

Have we not chiefs, tranfcending far
The old fam'd *thunderbolts of war ;*
Beyond the brave romantic fighters,
Stil'd *fwords of death* by novel-writers ?
Nor in romancing ages e'er rofe
So terrible a tier of heroes.
From Gage, what flafhes fright the waves !
How loud a blunderbufs is Graves * !
How Newport dreads the bluft'ring fallies,
That thunder from our popgun, Wallace *,
While noife in formidable ftrains
Spouts from his thimble-full of brains !
I fee you fink with aw'd furprize !
I fee our Tory-brethren rife !
And as the fect'ries Sandimanian †,
Our friends, defcribe their wifh'd Millennium ;
Tell how the world in ev'ry region
At once fhall own their true religion ;
For Heav'n with plagues of awful dread
Shall knock all heretics o' th' head ;

---

* Admiral Graves and Captain Wallace lay before the town
of Newport a long time, and by their " Deeds above heroic,"
merited all the praifes that the difcerning M'Fingal has here
beftowed upon them.                                Edit.

† The religious fect of Sandimanians, and their fingular ideas
of the Millennium are well known in this country.  In Ame-
rica, their political religion was Toryifm.        Edit.

And

And then their church, the meek in fpirit,
The earth, as promis'd, fhall inherit,
From the dead wicked, as heirs-male,
And next remainder-men in tail:
Such ruin fhall the Whigs opprefs!
Such fpoils our Tory friends fhall blefs!
While Confifcation at command
Shall ftalk in horror thro' the land,
Shall give your Whig-eftates away,
And call our brethren into play.

    " And can ye doubt or fcruple more,
Thefe things are near you at the door?
Behold! for tho' to reas'ning blind,
Signs of the times ye fure might mind,
And view impending fate as plain
As ye'd foretell a fhow'r of rain.

    " Hath not Heav'n warn'd you what muft enfue,
And Providence declar'd againft you;
Hung forth its dire portents of war,
By * figns and beacons in the air;
Alarm'd old women all around
By fearful noifes under ground;
While earth for many dozen leagues
Groan'd with her difmal load of Whigs?

---

* Such ftories of prodigies were at that time induftriously
propagated by the Tory-party in various parts of New-Eng-
land, to terrify and intimidate the fuperftitious.

                                  Was

Was there a meteor far and wide
But mufter'd on the Tory-fide ?
A ftar malign that has not bent
Its afpects for the Parliament,
Foreboding your defeat and mifery ;
As once they fought againft old Sifera ?
Was there a cloud that fpread the fkies,
But bore our armies of allies ?
While dreadful hofts of fire ftood forth
'Mid baleful glimm'rings from the North * ;
Which plainly fhows which part they join'd,
For North's the minifter, ye mind ;
Whence oft your quibblers in gazettes
On *Northern blafts* have ftrain'd their wits ;
And think ye not the clouds know how
To make the pun as well as you ?
Did there arife an apparition,
But grinn'd forth ruin to fedition ?
A death-watch, but has join'd our leagues,
And click'd deftruction to the Whigs ?

---

* It is faid to be a fact, that in America, about the com-
mencement of the war, the *aurora borealis* appeared more fre-
quently than ufual, and affumed more fingular appearances.
Our hero's reafoning on this phænomenon is precifely that of
many of his countrymen of that day ; and there is no doubt
but the government of Great-Britain gained many fubftantial
profelytes and friends, from the mere circumftance of the or-
thography of the *name* of the minifter, whom our gracious
Sovereign appointed to conduct that glorious war. *Edit.*

I                           Heard

Heard ye not, when the wind was fair,
At night our or'tors in the air,
That, loud as admiralty-libel,
Read awful chapters from the bible,
And death and deviltry denounc'd,
And told you how you'd foon be trounc'd?
I fee, to join our conqu'ring fide
Heav'n, earth, and hell at once allied!
See from your overthrow and end
The Tories paradife afcend ;
Like that new world that claims its flation
Beyond the final conflagration !
I fee the day that lots your fhare
In utter darknefs and defpair ;
The day of joy, when North, our Lord,
His faithful fav'rites fhall reward !
No Tory then fhall fet before him
Small wifh of 'Squire, or Juftice Quorum ,
But 'fore his unmiftaken eyes
See Lordfhips, pofts and penfions rife.
Awake to gladnefs then, ye Tories,
Th' unbounded profpect lies before us :
The pow'r difplay'd in Gage's banners
Shall cut Amer'can lands to manors,
And o'er our happy conquer'd ground
Difpenfe eftates and titles round.

Behold.

Behold, the world fhall ftare at new fets
Of home-made * earls in Maffachufetts;
Admire, array'd in ducal taffels,
Your Ol'vers, Hutchinfons, and Vaffals;
See, join'd in minifterial work,
His grace of Albany and York!
What Lordfhips from each carv'd eftate,
On our New-York Affembly wait!
What titled † Jauncys, Gales, and Billops;
Lord Brufh, Lord Wilkins, and Lord Phillips!
In wide-fleev'd pomp of godly guife,
What folemn rows of bifhops rife!
Aloft a card'nal's hat is fpread
O'er punfter ‡ Cooper's rev'rend head!
In Vardell, that poetic zealot,
I view a lawn-bedizen'd prelate!
While mitres fall, as 'tis their duty,
On heads of Chandler and Auchmuty!
Knights, vifcounts, barons, fhall ye meet,
As thick as pavements in the ftreet!

* See Hutchinfon's and Oliver's Letters.

† Members of the minifterial Majority in the New-York
Affembly; Wilkins, a noted writer.

‡ Prefident Cooper is a notorious punfter: Vardell, author
of fome poetical fatires on the fons of liberty in New-York,
and royal profeffor in King's college; Chandler and Auch-
muty, High-church and Tory-writers of the clerical order.

Ev'n

Ev'n I, perhaps, Heav'n speed my claim,
Shall fix a *Sir* before my name.
For titles all our foreheads ache;
For what bleft changes can they make!
Place rev'rence, grace, and excellence
Where neither claim'd the leaft pretence;
Transform by patent's magic words
Men, likeft Devils, into Lords;
Whence commoners, to peers tranflated,
Are juftly faid to be *created!*
Now where commiffioners ye faw
Shall boards of nobles deal you law!
Long-rob'd comptrollers judge your rights,
And tide-waiters ftart up in knights!
While Whigs fubdu'd in flavifh awe,
Our wood fhall hew, our water draw,
And blefs that mildnefs, when paft hope,
Which fav'd their necks from noofe of rope.
For as to gain affiftance we
Defign their Negroes to fet free;
For Whigs, when we enough fhall bang 'em,
Perhaps 'tis better not to hang 'em;
Except their chiefs; the vulgar knaves
Will do more good preferv'd for flaves."

    " 'Tis well, Honorius cried, your fcheme
Has painted out a pretty dream.
We can't confute your fecond fight;
We fhall be flaves and you a knight:

                           Thefe

Thefe things muft come : but I divine
They'll come not in your day, or mine.
But oh, my friends, my brethren, hear,
And turn for once th' attentive ear.
Ye fee how prompt to aid our woes,
The tender mercies of our foes;
Ye fee with what unvaried rancour
Still for our blood their minions hanker,
Nor aught can fate their mad ambition,
From us, but death, or worfe, fubmiffion.
Shall thefe then riot in our fpoil,
Reap the glad harveft of our toil,
Rife from their country's ruin proud,
And roll their chariot wheels in blood?
And can ye fleep while high outfpread
Hangs defolation o'er your head?
See Gage with inaufpicious ftar.
Has op'd the gates of civil war;
When ftreams of gore from freemen flain,
Encrimfon'd Concord's fatal plain;
Whofe warning voice, with awful found,
Still cries, like Abel's, from the ground,
And Heav'n, attentive to its call,
Shall doom the proud oppreffor's fall."
    " Rife then, ere ruin fwift furprize,
To victory, to vengeance rife!
Mark, how the diftant din alarms!
The echoing trumpet breathes, to arms;

3

From

From provinces remote, afar,
The fons of glory rouze to war;
'Tis freedom calls; th' enraptur'd found
The Apalachian hills rebound;
The Georgian fhores her voice fhall hear,
And ftart from lethargies of fear.
From the parch'd zone, with glowing ray,
Where pours the fun intenfer day,
To fhores where icy waters roll,
And tremble to the dufky pole,
Infpir'd by freedom's heav'nly charms,
United nations wake to arms.
The ftar of conqueft lights their way,
And guides their vengeance on their prey—
Yes, tho' tyrannic force oppofe,
Still fhall they triumph o'er their foes,
Till Heav'n the happy land fhall blefs,
With fafety, liberty, and peace."

　　" And ye whofe fouls of daftard mould
Start at the brav'ry of the bold;
To love your country who pretend,
Yet want all fpirit to defend;
Who feel your fancies fo prolific,
Engend'ring vifion'd whims terrific,
O'er-run with horrors of coercion,
Fire, blood, and thunder in reverfion,
King's ftandards, pill'ries, confifcations,
And Gage's fcare-crow proclamations,

　　　　　　　　　　　　　　With

With all the trumpery of fear;
Hear bullets whizzing in your rear;
Who fcarce could rouze, if caught in fray,
Prefence of mind to run away;
See nought but halters rife to view
In all your dreams, (and dreams are true;)
And while thefe phantoms haunt your brains,
Bow down the willing neck to chains.
Heav'ns! are ye fons of fires fo great,
Immortal in the fields of fate,
Who brav'd all deaths by land or fea,
Who bled, who conquer'd to be free!
Hence! coward fouls, the worft difgrace
Of our forefathers' valiant race;
Hie homeward from the glorious field;
There turn the wheel, the diftaff wield;
Act what ye are, nor dare to ftain
The warrior's arms with touch profane:
There beg your more heroic wives
To guard your children and your lives;
Beneath their aprons find a fcreen,
Nor dare to mingle more with men."
  " As thus he faid, the Tories' anger
Could now reftrain itfelf no longer,
Who tried before by many a freak, or
Infulting noife, to ftop the fpeaker;
Swung th' unoil'd hinge of each pew-door;
Their feet kept fhuffling on the floor;

                                  Made

Made their difapprobation known
By many a murmur, hum, and groan,
That to his fpeech fupplied the place
Of counterpart in thorough-bafe:
As bag-pipes, while the tune they breathe,
Still drone and grumble underneath;
Or as the fam'd Demofthenes
Harangu'd the rumbling of the feas,
Held forth with eloquence full grave
To audience loud of wind and wave;
And had a ftiller congregation
Than Tories are to hear th' oration.
But now the ftorm grew high and louder,
As nearer thundrings of a cloud are,
And ev'ry foul with heart and voice
Supplied his quota of the noife;
Each lift'ning ear was fet on torture
Each Tory bell'wing out, to order;
And fome, with tongue not low or weak,
Were clam'ring faft, for leave to fpeak;
The moderator, with great vi'lence,
The cufhion thump'd with " Silence! filence!"
The conftable to ev'ry prater
Bawl'd out, " Pray hear the moderator;"
Some call'd the vote, and fome, in turn,
Were fcreaming high, " Adjourn, adjourn."
Not chaos heard fuch jars and clafhes
When all the el'ments fought for places.

                                    Each

Each bludgeon foon for blows was tim'd ;
Each fift ftood ready cock'd and prim'd ;
The ftorm each moment louder grew ;
His fword the great M'Fingal drew,
Prepar'd in either chance to fhare,
To keep the peace, or aid the war.
Nor lack'd they each poetic being,
Whom bards alone are fkill'd in feeing ;
Plum'd Victory ftood perch'd on high,
Upon the pulpit-canopy,
To join, as is her cuftom tried,
Like Indians, on the ftrongeft fide ;
The Deftinies with fhears and diftaff,
Drew near, their threads of life to twift off ;
The Furies 'gan to feaft on blows,
And broken heads or bloody nofe ;
When on a fudden, from without,
Arofe a loud terrific fhout ;
And ftrait the people all at once heard
Of tongues an univerfal concert ;
Like Æfop's times, as fable runs,
When ev'ry creature talk'd at once ;
Or like the variegated gabble
That craz'd the carpenters of Babel.
Each party foon forgot the quarrel,
And let the other go on parole ;
Eager to know what fearful matter
Had conjur'd up fuch gen'ral clatter ;

K                           And

And left the church in thin array,
As tho' it had been lecture-day.
Our 'Squire M'Fingal ftraitway beckon'd
The conftable to ftand his fecond,
And fallied forth with afpect fierce
The croud affembled to difperfe.
The moderator, out of view
Beneath a bench, had lain perdue;
Peep'd up his head to view the fray,
Beheld the wranglers run away,
And, left alone, with folemn face,
Adjourn'd them without time or place.

END OF CANTO SECOND.

# M'FINGAL:

## CANTO THIRD.

## *The Liberty-Pole.*

NOW arm'd with minifterial ire,
   Fierce fallied forth our loyal 'Squire,
And on his ftriding fteps attends,
His defp'rate clan of Tory friends;
When fudden met his angry eye,
A pole afcending thro' the fky,
Which num'rous throngs of Whiggifh race
Were raifing in the market-place;
Not higher fchool-boys kites afpire,
Or royal maft, or country fpire,

Like fpears at Brobdignagian tilting,
Or Satan's walking-ftaff in Milton;
And on its top the flag unfurl'd,
Wav'd triumph o'er the proftrate world,
Infcrib'd with inconfiftent types
Of *liberty* and *thirteen ftripes* *.
Beneath, the croud, without delay,
The dedication-rites effay,
And gladly pay, in ancient fafhion,
The ceremonies of libation;
While brifkly to each patriot lip
Walks eager round th' infpiring fiip †:
Delicious draught, whofe pow'rs inherit
The quinteffence of public fpirit!
Which whofo taftes, perceives his mind
To nobler politics refin'd,
Or rouz'd for martial controverfy,
As from transforming cups of Circe;
Or warm'd with Homer's nectar'd liquor,
That fill'd the veins of gods with ichor.
At hand for new fupplies in ftore,
The tavern opes its friendly door,
Whence to and fro the waiters run,
Like bucket-men, at fires in town.

* *Thirteen ftripes*, the American flag. *Edit.*

† *Flip* is a liquor compofed of beer, rum, and fugar. The
Poet fuppofes large drafts of this liquor to be ufed in the dedi-
cation of the Liberty Pole; which fhows that he is not un-
acquainted with the people whofe manners he defcribes. *Edit.*

I                                              Then

Then with three fhouts that tore the fky,
'Tis confecrate to Liberty ;
To guard it from th' attacks of Tories,
A grand committee cull'd of four is,
Who, foremoft on the patriot fpot,
Had brought the flip and paid the fhot.

By this, M'Fingal, with his train,
Advanc'd upon th' adjacent plain,
And fierce, with loyal rage poffefs'd,
Pour'd forth the zeal, that fir'd his breaft.
" What mad-brain'd rebel gave commiffion,
To raife this May-pole of fedition !
Like Babel rear'd by bawling throngs,
With like confufion too of tongues,
To point at Heav'n, and fummon down
The thunders of the Britifh crown ?
Say, will this paltry pole fecure
Your forfeit heads from Gage's pow'r ?
Attack'd by heroes brave and crafty,
Is this to ftand your ark of fafety ?
Or driv'n by Scottifh laird and laddie,
Think ye to reft beneath its fhadow ?
When bombs, like fiery ferpents, fly,
And balls move hiffing thro' the fky,  ·
Will this vile pole, devote to freedom,
Save like the Jewifh pole in Edom,
Or like the brazen fnake of Mofes,
Cure your crackt fkulls and batter'd nofes ?

Ye

Ye dupes to ev'ry factious rogue,
Or tavern-prating demagogue,
Whose tongue but rings, with sound more full,
On th' empty drumhead of his skull;
Behold you not what noisy fools
Use you, worse simpletons, for tools?
For Liberty in your own by-sense
Is but for crimes a patent licence;
To break of law th' Egyptian yoke,
And throw the world in common stock,
Reduce all grievances and ills
To Magna Charta of your wills,
Establish cheats and frauds and nonsense,
Fram'd by the model of your conscience,
Cry justice down, as out of fashion,
And fix its scale of depreciation *,
Defy all creditors to trouble ye,
And pass new years of Jewish jubilee;
Drive judges out, like Aaron's calves,
By jurisdiction of white staves,
And make the bar and bench and steeple,
Submit t' our sov'reign Lord, the People;
Assure each knave his whole assets,
By gen'ral amnesty of debts;

* Alluding to the depreciation of the continental paper-money. The declining value of this Currency was ascertained and declared by Congress, in what was called *a scale of depreciation.* See more of this subject in the last Canto.  *Edit.*

By

By plunder rife to pow'r and glory,
And brand all property as Tory;
Expofe all wares to lawful feizures
Of mobbers and monopolizers;
Break heads and windows and the peace,
For your own int'reft and increafe;
Difpute and pray and fight and groan,
For public good, and mean your own;
Prevent the laws, by fierce attacks,
From quitting fcores upon your backs,
Lay your old dread, the gallows, low,
And feize the ftocks, your ancient foe;
And turn them, as convenient engines
To wreak your patriotic vengeance;
While all, your claims who underftand,
Confefs they're in the owner's hand:
And when by clamours and confufions,
Your freedom's grown a public nuifance,
Cry, *Liberty*, with pow'rful yearning,
As he does, *fire*, whofe houfe is burning,
Tho' he already has much more,
Than he can find occafion for.
While ev'ry dunce, that turns the plains,
Tho' bankrupt in eftate and brains,
By this new light transform'd to traitor,
Forfakes his plow, to turn dictator,
Starts an haranguing chief of Whigs,
And drags you by the ears, like pigs.

                                        All

All bluſter arm'd with factious licence,
Transform'd at once to politicians;
Each leather-apron'd clown, grown wiſe,
Preſents his forward face t' adviſe,
And tatter'd legiſlators meet
From ev'ry work-ſhop thro' the ſtreet;
His gooſe the tailor finds new uſe in,
To patch and turn the conſtitution;
The blackſmith comes with ſledge and grate,
To iron-bind the wheels of ſtate;
The quack forbears his patient's ſouſe,
To purge the Council and the Houſe;
The tinker quits his moulds and doxies,
To caſt aſſembly men at proxies.
From dunghills deep of ſable hue,
Your dirt-bred patriots ſpring to view,
To wealth and pow'r and penſion riſe,
Like new-wing'd maggots chang'd to flies;
And flutt'ring round in proud parade,
Strut in the robe, or gay cockade.
See * Ar—d quits, for ways more certain,
His bankrupt perj'ries for his fortune;

                                   Brews

* Ar—d's perjuries at the time of his pretended bankrupt-
cy, which was the firſt riſe of his fortune; and his curious law-
ſuit againſt a brother-ſkipper, who had charged him with hav-
ing caught the above-mentioned diſeaſe, by his connection with
a certain African princeſs in the Weſt-Indies, with its humour-
                                                        ou.

Brews rum no longer in his ftore,
Jockey and fkipper now no more;
Forfakes his warehoufes and docks,
And writs of flander for the pox,
And, purg'd by patriotifm from fhame,
Grows Gen'ral of the foremoft name.

\* *Hiatus.*

For in this ferment of the ftream,
The dregs have work'd up to the brim,
And by the rule of topfy-turvys,
The fkum ftands fwelling on the furface.
You've caus'd your pyramid t' afcend,
And fet on the little end;
Like Hudibras, your empire's made,
Whofe crupper had o'er-top'd his head;
You've pufh'd and turn'd the whole world up-
Side down, and got yourfelves a-top:
While all the great ones of your ftate,
Are crufh'd beneath the pop'lar weight;
Nor can you boaft this prefent hour,
The fhadow of the form of pow'r.

ous iffue, are matters, not I believe fo generally known, as the
other circumftances of his public and private character.

\* M'Fingal having here inferted the names and characters of
feveral great men, whom the public have not yet fully detected,
it is thought proper to omit fundry paragraphs of his fpeech,
in the prefent edition.

L                                    For

For what's your Congrefs *, or its end?
A Power t' advife and recommend;
To call for troops, adjuft your quotas,
And yet no foul is bound to notice;
To pawn your faith to th' utmoft limit,
But cannot bind you to redeem it,
And when in want, no more in them lies,
Than begging of your State-Affemblies;
Can utter oracles of dread,
Like Friar Bacon's brazen head;
But fhould a faction e'er difpute 'em,
Has ne'er an arm to execute 'em.
As tho' you chofe fupreme dictators,
And put them under confervators;
You've but purfu'd the felf-fame way,
With Shakefpeare's Trinclo in the play,

---

\* The author here, in a true ftrain of patriotic cenfure,
pointed out the principal defects in the firft federal Conftitution
of the United States; all which have been fince removed in the
New Conftitution, eftablifhed in the year 1789. So that the pro-
phecy below, *You'll ne'er have fenfe enough to mend it*, muft be
ranked among the other fage blunders of his fecond-fighted
Hero. But the great M'Fingal himfelf has the fatisfaction of
being kept in countenance by the whole galaxy of Statefmen
and Philofophers in Europe, who believe and teach, that no
people can have fenfe enough to make their own laws. Thefe
men may turn, in a future day, to this great luminary of Ame-
rican royalifm, and boaft at leaft of the honour *cum Platone er-
rare*.                                                          *Edit.*

I                                                        " You

" You shall be viceroys here, 'tis true,
But we'll be viceroys over you."
What wild confusion hence must ensue,
Tho' common danger yet cements you ;
So some wreck'd veffel, all in shatters,
Is held up by surrounding waters,
But stranded, when the preffure ceafes,
Falls, by its rottennefs, to pieces.
And fall it must—if wars were ended,
You'll ne'er have fenfe enough to mend it ;
But creeping on with low intrigues
Like vermin of an hundred legs,
Will find as short a life affign'd
As all things elfe of reptile kind.
Your Commonwealth's a common harlot,
The property of ev'ry varlet,
Which, now in tafte and full employ,
All forts admire, as all enjoy ;
But foon a batter'd ftrumpet grown,
You'll curfe and drum her out of town.
Such is the government you chofe.
For this you bade the world be foes,
For this, fo mark'd for diffolution,
You fcorn the Britifh conftitution ;
That conftitution, form'd by fages,
The wonder of all modern ages :
Which owns no failure in reality,
Except corruption and venality ;

And

And only proves the adage juſt,
That beſt things ſpoil'd, corrupt to worſt :
So man, ſupreme in mortal ſtation,
And mighty lord of this creation,
When once his corſe is dead as herring,
Becomes the moſt offenſive carrion,
And ſooner breeds the plague, 'tis found,
Than all beaſts rotting 'bove the ground.
Yet for this gov'rnment, to diſmay us,
You've call'd up Anarchy from Chaos,
With all the followers of her ſchool,
Uproar and Rage and wild Miſrule ;
For whom this rout of Whigs diſtracted
And ravings dire of ev'ry crack'd head ;
Theſe new-caſt legiſlative engines
Of country-muſters and conventions,
Committees vile of correſpondence,
And mobs, whoſe tricks have almoſt undone 's ;
While reaſon fails to check your courſe,
And loyalty's kick'd out of doors,
And folly, like inviting landlord,
Hoiſts on your poles her royal ſtandard.
While the king's friends in doleful dumps,
Have worn their courage to the ſtumps,
And leaving George in ſad diſaſter,
Moſt ſinfully deny their maſter.

What

What furies rag'd, when you in fea,
In fhape of Indians drown'd the tea *,
When your gay fparks, fatigu'd to watch it,
Affumed the moggifon and hatchet,
With wampom'd blankets hid their laces,
And, like their fweet-hearts, primed their faces:
While not a Red-coat dar'd oppofe,
And fcarce a Tory fhow'd his nofe;
While Hutchinfon for fure retreat,
Manœuvred to his country feat,
And thence affrighted in the fuds,
Stole off bare-headed thro' the woods!
Have you not rous'd your mobs to join,
And make Mandamus-men refign,
Call'd forth each duffil-drefs'd curmudgeon,
With dirty trowfers and white bludgeon,
Forc'd all our Councils thro' the land,
To yield their necks to your command ;
While palenefs marks their late difgraces
Thro' all their rueful length of faces?
Have you not caus'd as woful work
In loyal city of New-York †,
When all the rabble, well cockaded,
In triumph thro' the ftreets paraded ;

* The perfons who deftroyed the cargo of tea, above re-
ferred to, were difguifed in the habit of Indians.    *Edit.*

† There were fo many influential Tories in New-York, that
they at firft obtained a vote in favour of the Acts of Parli-
ament, and againft the proceedings of the firft Congrefs. *Edit.*

And

And mobb'd the Tories, fear'd their fpoufes,
And ranfack'd all the cuftom-houfes,
Made fuch a tumult, blufter, jarring,
That 'mid the clafh of tempefts warring,
Smith's weathercock, with veers forlorn *,
Could hardly tell which way to turn ;
Burnt effigies of th' Higher Powers,
Contriv'd in planetary hours,
As witches, with clay-images,
Deftroy or torture whom they pleafe ;
'Till fir'd with rage, th' ungrateful club
Spar'd not your beft friend, Belzebub,
O'er-look'd his favours, and forgot
The rev'rence due t' his cloven foot ;
And in the felf-fame furnace frying,
Burn'd him, and North, and Bute, and Tryon † ?
Did you not in as vile and fhallow way,
Fright our poor Philadelphian, ‡ Galloway,

* William Smith, formerly a lawyer in New-York. We
believe he is now a Chief-Juftice in one of the Canadas. *Edit.*

† Tryon, being now dead, is probably forgot. The Englifh
reader muft know that he was governor of New-York, and a
Britifh general during the war. He had the glory of burning
the towns of Fairfield and Norwalk, and of iffuing many pro-
clamations. The other perfonages that make up this *kettle of
fifh,* Bute, Belzebub, and North, are ftill living, and there-
fore want no explanation.                    *Edit.*

‡ Galloway began by being a flaming patriot. He is one
of the few men, who proved a traitor to his country, wrote
againft it, and ran away.                    *Edit.*

                                              Your

Your Congrefs when the daring ribald
Belied, berated, and befcribbled?
What ropes and halters did you fend,
Terrific emblems of his end,
Till, leaft he'd hang in more than effigy,
Fled in a fog the trembling refugee?
Now rifing in progreffion fatal,
Have you not ventur'd to give battle?
When treafon chac'd our heroes troubled,
With rufty gun and leathern doublet,
Turn'd all ftone-walls, and groves, and bufhes,
To batt'ries arm'd with blunderbuffes,
And with deep wounds, that fate portend,
Gaul'd many a Reg'lar's latter end,
Drove them to Bofton, as in jail,
Confin'd without main-prize or bail.
Were not thefe deeds enough betimes,
To heap the meafure of your crimes,
But in this loyal town and dwelling,
You raife thefe enfigns of rebellion?
'Tis done; fair Mercy fhuts her door;
And Vengeance now fhall fleep no more;
Rife then, my friends, in terror rife,
And wipe this fcandal from the fkies!
You'll fee their Dagon, tho' well jointed,
Will fink before the Lord's anointed,
And like old Jericho's proud wall,
Before our ram's horns proftrate fall."

This

This faid our 'Squire, yet undifmay'd,
Call'd forth the Conftable to aid,
And bade him read in nearer ftation,
The riot-act and proclamation * ;
Who, now advancing tow'rd the ring,
Began, " Our fov'reign Lord the King"—
When thoufand clam'rous tongues he hears,
And clubs and ftones affail his ears ;
To fly was vain, to fight was idle,
By foes encompafs'd in the middle ;
In ftratagem his aid he found,
And fell right craftily to ground ;
Then crept to feek an hiding place,
'Twas all he could, beneath a brace ;
Where foon the conqu'ring crew efpied him,
And where he lurk'd, they caught and tied him.

At once with refolution fatal,
Both Whigs and Tories rufh'd to battle ;
Inftead of weapons, either band
Seiz'd on fuch arms, as came to hand.
And as fam'd † Ovid paints th' adventures
Of wrangling Lapithæ and Centaurs,

---

* *Reading the Riot-act* has the fame miraculous effect in
America as in England: it may convert any collection of men
into a *riot*, and is the tremendous prologue to any tragedy
that may refult from the exercife of Martial Law.       *Edit.*

† Ovid's Metamorphofes, Book xii.

Who at their feaft, by Bacchus led,
Threw bottles at each other's head,
And thefe arms failing in their fcuffles,
Attack'd with hand-irons, tongs, and fhovels :
So clubs and billets, ftaves and ftones
Met fierce, encount'ring ev'ry fconce,
And cover'd o'er with knobs and pains
Each void receptacle for brains ;
Their clamours rend the hills around,
And earth rebellows with the found ;
And many a groan increas'd the din
From broken nofe and batter'd fhin.
M'Fingal, rifing at the word,
Drew forth his old militia fword ;
Thrice cried, " King George," as erft in diftrefs
Romancing heroes did their miftrefs,
And, brandifhing the blade in air,
Struck terror thro' th' oppofing war.
The Whigs, unfafe within the wind
Of fuch commotion, fhrunk behind.
With whirling fteel around addrefs'd,
Fierce thro' their thickeft throng he prefs'd,
(Who roll'd on either fide in arch,
Like Red-fea waves in Ifrael's march)
And like a meteor rufhing through,
Struck on their pole a vengeful blow.
Around, the Whigs, of clubs and ftones
Difcharg'd whole vollies in platoons,

M                          That

That o'er in whiſtling terror fly,
But not a foe dares venture nigh.
And now, perhaps, with conqueſt crown'd,
Our 'Squire had fell'd their pole to ground;
Had not ſome Pow'r, a Whig at heart,
Deſcended down and took their part,
(Whether 'twere Pallas, Mars, or Iris,
'Tis ſcarce worth while to make enquiries,)
Who at the nick of time alarming,
Aſſum'd the graver form of Chairman;
Addreſs'd a Whig, in ev'ry ſcene
The ſtouteſt wreſtler on the green,
And pointed where the ſpade was found,
Late us'd to fix the pole in ground,
And urg'd with equal arms and might
To dare our 'Squire to ſingle fight *.
The Whig thus arm'd, untaught to yield,
Advanc'd tremendous to the field;
Nor did M'Fingal ſhun the foe,
But ſtood to brave the deſp'rate blow;
While all the party gaz'd ſuſpended,
To ſee the deadly combat ended.
And Jove in equal balance weigh'd
The ſword againſt the brandiſh'd ſpade,

* The learned reader will readily obſerve the alluſions in this
ſcene to the ſingle combat of Paris and Menelaus in Homer,
Æneas and Turnus in Virgil, and Michael and Satan in
Milton.

He

He weigh'd ; but lighter than a dream,
The fword flew up and kick'd the beam.
Our 'Squire on tiptoe rifing fair,
Lifts high a noble ftroke in air,
Which hung not, but like dreadful engines
Defcended on the foe in vengeance.
But ah ! in danger with difhonour,
The fword perfidious fails its owner ;
That fword, which oft had ftood its ground
By huge train-bands encompafs'd round *,
Or on the bench, with blade right loyal,
Had won the day at many a trial,
Of ftones and clubs had brav'd th' alarms,
Shrunk from thefe new Vulcanian arms.
The fpade fo temper'd from the fledge,        .
Nor keen nor folid harm'd its edge,
Now met it from his arm of might
Defcending with fteep force to fmite ;
The blade fnapp'd fhort—and from his hand
With ruft embrown'd the glitt'ring fand.
Swift turn'd M'Fingal at the view,
And call'd for aid th' attendant crew,
In vain ; the Tories all had run,
When fcarce the fight was well begun ;
Their fetting wigs he faw decreas'd,
Far in th' horizon tow'rd the weft.

* A *train-band* is a Captain's company in the Militia.  The
word is particularly applicable to fuch a company, when pa-
raded for manual exercife.                          *Edit.*

M 2                                  Amaz'd

Amaz'd he view'd the shameful fight,
And saw no refuge but in flight:
But age unweildy check'd his pace,
Tho' fear had wing d his flying race;
For not a trifling prize at stake;
No less than great M'Fingal's back.
With legs and arms he work'd his courfe,
Like rider that outgoes his horfe,
And labour'd hard to get away, as
Old Satan * struggling on thro' Chaos:
Till, looking back, he spied in rear
The spade arm'd chief advanc'd too near.
Then stopp'd and seiz'd a stone that lay,
An antient land-mark near the way;
Nor shall we, as old Bards have done,
Affirm it weigh'd an hundred ton:
But such a stone as at a shift
A modern might suffice to lift.
Since men, to credit their enigmas,
Are dwindled down to dwarfs and pigmies;
And giants, exil'd with their cronies,
To Brobdingnags and Patagonias.
But while our hero turn'd him round,
And stoop'd to raise it from the ground,
The deadly spade difcharg'd a blow
Tremendous on his rear below:
His bent knee fail'd, and void of strength,
Stretch'd on the ground his manly length;

* In Milton.

Like

Like antient oak o'er-turn'd he lay,
Or tow'rs to tempefts fall'n a prey,
And more things elfe—but all men know 'em,
If flightly vers'd in Epic Poem.
At once the crew, at this fad crifis,
Fall on, and bind him ere he rifes,
And with loud fhouts, and joyful foul,
Conduct him pris'ner to the pole.
   When now the Mob in lucky hour,
Had got their en'mies in their pow'r,
They firft proceed, by wife command,
To take the conftable in hand.
Then from the pole's fublimeft top
They fpeeded to let down the rope,
At once its other end in hafte bind,
And make it faft upon his waiftband,
Till, like the earth, as ftretch'd on tenter,
He hung felf-balanc'd on his center.
Then upwards, all hands hoifting fail,
They fwung him, like a keg of ale;
Till to the pinnacle fo fair,
He rofe like meteor in the air :
As * Socrates of old at firft did
To aid philofophy get hoifted,
And found his thoughts flow ftrangely clear,
Swung in a bafket in mid air :

* Socrates is reprefented in Ariftophanes's Comedy of the
Clouds, as hoifted in a bafket to aid contemplation.

Our

Our culprit thus in purer fky,
With like advantage rais'd his eye;
And look g forth in profpect wide
His Tory errors clearly fpied,
And from his elevated ftation,
With bawling voice began addreffing.
" Good gentlemen, and friends, and kin,
For Heav'n's fake hear, if not for mine!
I here renounce the Pope, the Turks,
The King, the Devil, and all their works;
And will, fet me but once at eafe,
Turn Whig or Chriftian, what you pleafe;
And always mind your laws as juftly;
Should I live long as old Methus'lah,
I'll never join with Britifh rage,
Nor help Lord North, or Gen'ral Gage,
Nor lift my gun in future fights,
Nor take away your charter'd rights;
Nor overcome your new-rais'd levies,
Deftroy your towns, nor burn your navies;
Nor cut your poles down while I've breath,
Tho' rais'd more thick than hatchel teeth:
But leave king George and all his elves
To do their conqu'ring work themfelves."
    This faid, they lower'd him down in ftate,
Spread at all points, like falling cat;
But took a vote firft on the queftion,
That they'd accept this full confeffion,

And

And to their fellowſhip and favour,
Reſtore him on his good behaviour.

  Not ſo, our 'Squire ſubmits to rule,
But ſtood heroic as a mule.
" You'll find it all in vain, quoth he,
To play your rebel tricks on me.
All puniſhments the world can render,
Serve only to provoke th' offender ;
The will's confirm'd by treatment horrid,
As hides grow harder when they're curri'd.
No man e'er felt the halter draw,
With good opinion of the law ;
Or held in method orthodox
His love of juſtice in the ſtocks ;
Or fail'd to loſe by ſheriff's ſhears
At once his loyalty and ears.
Have you made Murray look leſs big,
Or ſmoak'd old Williams to a Whig ?
Did our mobb'd * Oliver quit his ſtation,
Or heed his vows of reſignation ?

                                    Has

* This is the " Chief-Judge Oliver" of the firſt Canto, in
whoſe appointment the ſagacious M'Fingal perceives that Hea-
ven had no hand.   One ground of the quarrel between the
Britiſh government and the people of Maſſachuſetts, was the
act by which the Judges of the Colony were rendered indepen-
dent of the Colony for their ſalary, as well as for their places ;
which was contrary to ancient uſage.   When the people felt
theſe particular acts of oppreſſion from a power three thouſand
                                                            miles

Has Rivington \*, in dread of ftripes,
Ceas'd lying fince you ftole his types ?
And can you think my faith will alter,
By tarring, whipping, or the halter ?
I'll ftand the worft ; for recompence
I truft King George and Providence.
And when, our conqueft gain'd, I come,
Array'd in law and terror, home,
You'll rue this inaufpicious morn,
And curfe the day you e'er were born,
In Job's high ftyle of imprecations,
With all his plagues, without his patience."

miles diftant, their only method of redrefs was, to prevent any
perfon from accepting an office, or from exercifing its func-
tions, under fuch an act. This expedient had been fuccefsful
in the cafe of the Stamp-act a few years before ; and the peo-
ple now applied to Judge Oliver, requefting him to refign an
office, the new arrangement of which fo manifeftly ftruck at
the foundation of their liberty. The Judge promifed to re-
fign his place ; but afterwards claimed that " *higheft privilege
of fpeech,*" which M'Fingal has fo well vindicated in favour of
General Gage.                                          *Edit.*

  \* Here again is an old acquaintance of the firft Canto.
His paper, entitled *The Royal Gazette*, had, by a ftrange com-
bination of circumftances, obtained the name, through all the
country, of *The Lying Gazette*. It was on this account that
the people at a certain time fent a committee to take away his
types. But this meafure was as ineffectual as thofe that were
ufed with Murray, Williams, Oliver, &c.                *Edit.*

                             Meanwhile

Meanwhile, befide the pole, the guard
A Bench of Juftice had prepar'd,
Where, fitting round in awful fort,
The grand Committee hold their court;
While all the crew, in filent awe,
Wait from their lips the lore of law.
Few moments, with deliberation,
They hold the folemn confultation,
When foon in judgment all agree,
And Clerk declares the dread decree;
" That 'Squire M'Fingal having grown
The vileft Tory in the town,
And now on full examination,
Convicted by his own confeffion,
Finding no tokens of repentance,
This Court proceed to render fentence:
That firft the Mob a flip-knot fingle .
Tie round the neck of faid M'Fingal;
And in due form do tar him next,
And feather, as the law directs;
Then thro' the town attendant ride him,
In cart, with Conftable befide him;
And having held him up to fhame,
Bring to the pole from whence he came."
    Forthwith the crowd proceed to deck,
With halter'd noofe, M'Fingal's neck,
While he, in peril of his foul,
Stood tied half-hanging to the pole;

N                              Then

Then lifting high the pond'rous jar,
Pour'd o'er his head the fmoaking tar:
With lefs profufion erft was fpread
The Jewifh oil on royal head,
That down his beard and veftments ran,
And cover'd all his outward man.
As when (fo * Claudian fings) the gods
And earth-born giants fell at odds,
The ftout Enceladus in malice
Tore mountains up to throw at Pallas;
And as he held them o'er his head,
The river from their fountains fed,
Pour'd down his back its copious tide,
And wore its channels in his hide:
So from the high rais'd urn the torrents,
Spread down his fide their various currents;
His flowing wig, as next the brim,
Firft met and drank the fable ftream;
Adown his vifage, ftern and grave,
Roll'd and adhered the vifcid wave;
With arms depending as he ftood,
Each cuff capacious holds the flood;
From nofe and chin's remoteft end,
The tarry icicles depend;
Till all o'erfpread, with colours gay
He glitter'd to the weftern ray,

* Claudian's Gigantomachia.

Like

Like fleet-bound trees in wintry fkies,
Or Lapland idol carv'd in ice.
And now the feather-bag difplay'd,
Is wav'd in triumph o'er his head,
And fpread him o'er with feathers miffive,
And down, upon the tar adhefive:
Not Maia's fon, with wings for ears,
Such plumes around his vifage wears;
Nor Milton's fix-wing'd angel gathers,
Such fuperfluity of feathers.
Till all compleat appears our 'Squire
Like Gorgon or Chimera dire;
Nor more could boaft on * Plato's plan
To rank amid the race of man,
Or prove his claim to human nature,
As a two-legg'd, unfeather'd creature.

Then on the two-wheel'd car of ftate,
They rais'd our grand Duumvirate.
And as at Rome a like committee,
That found an owl within their city,
With folemn rites and fad proceffions,
At ev'ry fhrine perform'd luftrations;
And left infection fhould abound,
From prodigy with face fo round,
All Rome attends him thro' the ftreet,
In triumph to his country-feat:

* Alluding to Plato's famous definition of Man, " *Animal
bipes, implumis.*"

N 2                                    With

With like devotion all the choir
Paraded round our feather'd 'Squire;
In front the martial mufic comes
Of horns and fiddles, fifes and drums,
With jingling found of carriage bells,
And treble creak of rufted wheels;
Behind, the crowd in lengthen'd row,
With grave proceffion clos'd the fhow;
And at fit periods ev'ry throat
Combin'd in univerfal fhout,
And hail'd great Liberty in chorus,
Or bawl'd, Confufion to the Tories.
Not louder ftorm the welkin braves,
From clamors of conflicting waves;
Lefs dire in Lybian wilds the noife
When rav'ning lions lift their voice;
Or triumphs at town-meetings made,
On pafling votes to reg'late trade *.

　　Thus having borne them round the town,
Laft at the pole they fet them down,
And tow'rd the tavern take their way,
To end in mirth the feftal day.

　　And now the Mob, difpers'd and gone,
Left 'Squire and Conftable alone.

----

\* Such votes were frequently paffed at Town-meetings;
the object of which was, to prevent the augmentation of
prices on the neceffaries of life, and thus to obviate the effects
of the depreciation of the paper-money.　　　*Edit.*

The

The Conftable, in rueful cafe,
Lean'd fad and folemn o'er a brace,
And faft befide him, cheek by jowl,
Stuck 'Squire M'Fingal 'gainft the pole,
Glu'd by the tar, t' his rear applied,
Like barnacle on veffel's fide:
But tho' his body lack'd phyfician,
His fpirit was in worfe condition.
He found his fears of whips and ropes,
By many a drachm out-weigh'd his hopes.
As men in gaol without mainprize,
View ev'ry thing with other eyes;
And all goes wrong in church and ftate,
Seen thro' perfpective of the grate:
So now M'Fingal's fecond-fight
Beheld all things in diff'rent light;
His vifual nerve, well purg'd with tar,
Saw all the coming fcenes of war.
As his prophetic foul grew ftronger,
He found he could hold in no longer;
Firft from the pole, as fierce he fhook,
His wig from pitchy durance broke,
His mouth unglu'd, his feathers flutter'd,
His tarr'd fkirts crack'd, and thus he utter'd:
" Ah, Mr. Conftable, in vain
We ftrive 'gainft wind, and tide, and rain!
Behold my doom! this feather'd omen
Portends what difmal times are coming.

                                        Now

Now future fcenes before my eyes,
And fecond-fighted forms arife;
I hear a voice that calls away,
And cries, the Whigs will win the day;
My beck'ning Genius gives command,
And bids us fly the fatal land;
Where, changing name and conftitution,
Rebellion turns to Revolution,
While Loyalty, opprefs'd in tears,
Stands trembling for its neck and ears.
Go, fummon all our brethren greeting,
To mufter at our ufual meeting.
There my prophetic voice fhall warn 'em,
Of all things future that concern 'em,
And fcenes difclofe, on which, my friend,
Their conduct and their lives depend:
There I—but firft 'tis more of ufe,
From this vile pole to fet me loofe;——
Then go with cautious fteps and fteady,
While I fteer home and make all ready."

**END OF CANTO THIRD.**

# M'FINGAL:

## CANTO FOURTH.

## *The Vision.*

NOW night came down, and rofe full foon
That patronefs of rogues, the Moon;
Beneath whofe kind, protecting ray,
Wolves, brute and human, prowl for prey.
The honeft world all fnored in chorus,
While owls, and ghofts, and thieves and Tories,
Whom erft the mid-day fun had aw'd,
Crept from their lurking holes abroad.
On cautious hinges, flow and ftiller
Wide ope'd the great M'Fingal's * cellar,

---

* Panditur interea domus omnipotentis Olympi,
  Conciliumq; vocat Divum pater atq; hominum rex
  Sideream in fedem.　　　　Lib. 10. Æneid.

'Where,

Where, shut from prying eyes in cluster,
The Tory Pandemonium muster.
Their chiefs all sitting round descry'd are,
On kegs of ale, and seats of cyder;
When first M'Fingal, dimly seen,
Rose solemn from the turnip-bin.
Nor yet his * form had wholly lost
The orig'nal brightness it could boast,
Nor less appear'd than Justice Quorum,
In feather'd majesty before 'em.
Adown his tar-streak'd visage, clear
Fell glist'ning fast th' indignant tear,
And thus his voice, in mournful wise,
Pursu'd the prologue of his sighs:
   " Brethren and friends, the glorious band
Of loyalty in rebel land!
It was not thus you've seen me sitting
Return'd in triumph from town-meeting,
When blust'ring Whigs were put to stand,
And votes obey'd my guiding hand,
And new commissions pleas'd my eyes;
Blest days, but, ah, no more to rise!
Alas! against my better light
And optics sure of second-sight,
My stubborn soul, in error strong,
Had faith in Hutchinson too long.

* —— His form had not yet lost
   All its original brightness, nor appear'd
   Less than Archangel ruin'd.                *Milton.*

3                                          See

See what brave trophies ſtill we bring
From all our battles for the king;
And yet theſe plagues, now paſt before us,
Are but our entring-wedge of ſorrows.
I ſee, in glooms tempeſtuous, ſtand
The cloud impending o'er the land;
That cloud, which ſtill beyond their hopes
Serves all our orators with tropes,
Which tho' from our own vapors fed,
Shall point its thunders on our head!
I ſee the Mob, beflipp'd in taverns,
Hunt us, like wolves, thro' wilds and caverns!
What dungeons riſe t' alarm our fears!
What horſe-whips whiſtle round our ears!
Tar, yet in embryo in the pine,
Shall run, on Tories backs to ſhine;
Trees rooted fair in groves of ſallows
Are growing for our future gallows;
And geeſe unhatch'd, when pluck'd in fray,
Shall rue the feath'ring of that day.
For me, before theſe fatal days,
I mean to fly th' accurſed place,
And follow omens, which of late
Have warn'd me of impending fate;
Yet paſs'd unnotic'd o'er my view,
Till ſad conviction prov'd them true;
As prophecies of beſt intent,
Are only heeded in th' event.

O                          For

For late in visions of the night
The gallows stood before my sight;
I saw its ladder heav'd on end;
I saw the deadly rope descend;
And in its noose, that wav'ring swang,
Friend * Malcolm hung, or seem'd to hang.
How changed from him, who, bold as lion,
Stood Aid-de-Camp to Governor Tryon,
Made rebels vanish once, like witches,
And sav'd his life, but dropp'd his breeches.
I scarce had made a fearful bow,
And trembling ask'd him, "How d'ye do?"
When hung up his eyes so wide,
His eyes alone, his hands were tied;
With feeble voice, as spirits use,
Now almost choak'd with gripe of noose;

---

* Malcolm was a Scotchman, Aid to Governor Tryon in
his expedition against the Regulators in North-Carolina, where,
in the engagement, he met with the accident of the breeches
here alluded to. He was afterwards an under-officer of the
customs in Boston, where becoming obnoxious, he was tarred,
feathered, and half-hanged by the mob, about the year 1774.
After this he was neglected and avoided by his own party, and
thinking his merits and sufferings unrewarded, appeared equal-
ly malevolent against Whigs and Tories.

The pretences of the Highlanders to prophecy by second-
sight, are too well known to need an explanation.

"Ah

" Ah, * fly, my friend ! he cri'd ; efcape !
And keep yourfelf from this fad fcrape ;
Enough you've talk'd, and writ, and plann'd ;
The Whigs have got the upper hand.
Dame Fortune's wheel has turn'd fo fhort,
It plung'd us fairly in the dirt ;
Could mortal arm our fears have ended,
This arm (and fhook it) had defended.
But longer now 'tis vain to ftay ;
See ev'n the Reg'lars run away :
Wait not till things grow defperater,
For hanging is no laughing matter :
This might your grandfires' fortunes tell you on,
Who both were hang'd the laft rebellion ;
Adventure then no longer ftay,
But call your friends and run away.
For lo, thro' deepeft glooms of night
I come to aid thy fecond-fight,
Difclofe the plagues that round us wait
And wake the dark decrees of Fate ;
Afcend this ladder, whence unfurl'd
The curtain opes of t' other world,
For here new worlds their fcenes unfold,
Seen from this back-door of the old †.

                                                    As

* There is in this fcene, a general allufion to the appearance
and fpeech of Hector's ghoft, in the fecond book of the Æneid.

† That the gallows is the *back-door* leading from this to the
                        O 2                        other

As when Æneas rifqu'd his life,
Like Orpheus vent'ring for his wife,
And bore in fhow his mortal carcafe,
Thro' realms of Erebus and Orcus,
Then in the happy fields Elyfian,
Saw all his embryon fons in vifion :
As, fhown by great archangel, Michael,
Old Adam faw the world's whole fequel,
And from the mount's extended fpace,
The rifing fortunes of his race ;
So from this ftage fhalt thou behold,
The war its coming fcenes unfold,
Rais'd by my arm to meet thine eye ;
My Adam, thou, thine Angel, I.
But firft my pow'r for vifions * bright,
Muft cleanfe from clouds thy mental fight,
Remove the dim fuffufions fpread,
Which bribes and fal'ries there have bred ;
And, from the well of Bute, infufe
Three genuine drops of Highland dews,
To purge, like euphrafy and rue,
Thine eyes, for much thou haft to view.
   " Now, freed from Tory darknefs, raife
Thy head, and fpy the coming days ;

other world, is a perfectly new idea in Epic Poetry ; unlefs
the hint might have been taken from the rear-trumpet of Fame
in our Hudibras.                                    *Edit.*
    * See Milton's Paradife Loft, Book 11.

                                                          For

For lo, before our fecond-fight,
The Continent afcends in light;
From north to fouth, what gath'ring fwarms,
Increafe the pride of rebel arms!
Thro' ev'ry State our legions brave,
Speed gallant marches to the grave,
Of battling Whigs the frequent prize,
While rebel trophies ftain the fkies.
Behold, o'er northern realms afar *,
Extend the kindling flames of war!

* Nothing lefs than the whole Hiftory of the American
War would be fufficient, completely to illuftrate the merits of
this fingle paragraph. Malcolm, the gallows-taught prophet,
in preparing the mind of M'Fingal to contemplate, with pro-
per intelligence, the various fcenes that are to rife fucceffively
to view in the courfe of the Vifion, glances over the Continent,
and mentions in this paffage the principal fcenes of action,
from the expedition into Canada in 1775, to the capture of
Lord Cornwallis in 1781. The concluding part of his fpeech
is therefore a kind of *argument* to this whole book of Vifion;
in which the fame objects are unfolded at large with their at-
tendant circumftances; in order that they may make a proper
impreffion on the elevated mind of the great M'Fingal. It is
thus that our Poet, like Homer, his illuftrious predeceffor,
feizes all occafions to do honour to his principal hero. By
fuppofing him already poffeffed of all natural and political
knowledge that could be obtained by mortal ftudy and expe-
rience, he makes him, like Achilles, capable of receiving in-
ftruction only by the agency of a fuper-terreftial power.
The advifers of Achilles defcended from the fkies, that of
M'Fingal is mounted towards the fkies. *Edit.*

See

See fam'd St. John's and Montreal,
Doom'd by Montgom'ry's arm to fall!
Where Hudfon with majeftic fway,
Thro' hills difparted plows his way ;
Fate fpreads on Bemus' Heights alarms,
And pours deftruction on our arms ;
There Bennington's enfanguin'd plain,
And Stony-Point, the prize of Wayne.
Behold near Del'ware's icy roar,
Where morning dawns on Trenton's fhore,
While Heffians fpread their Chriftmas fcails,
Rufh rude thefe uninvited guefts ;
Nor aught avail, to Whigs a prize,
Their martial whifkers' grifly fize.
On Princeton plains our heroes yield,
And fpread in flight the vanquifh'd field.
While fear to Mawhood's heels puts on
Wings, wide as worn by Maia's fon.
Behold the Pennfylvanian fhore,
Enrich'd with ftreams of Britifh gore ;
Where many a vet'ran chief in bed
Of honour refts his flumb'ring head,
And in foft vales in land of foes,
Their wearied virtue finds repofe.
See plund'ring Dunmore's negro band
Fly headlong from Virginia's ftrand ;
And far on fouthern hills, our coufins,
The Scotch M'Donalds, fall by dozens ;

                              Or

Or where King's Mountain lifts its head,
Our ruin'd bands in triumph led!
Behold o'er Tarleton's bluftring train,
The Rebels ftretch the captive chain!
Afar near Eutaw's fatal fprings
Defcending Vict'ry fpreads her wings!
Thro' all the land in various chace,
We hunt the rainbow of fuccefs;
In vain! their Chief, fuperior ftill,
Eludes our force with Fabian fkill;
Or fwift defcending by furprize,
Like Pruffia's eagle fweeps the prize."

　"I look'd, nor yet, oppreft with fears,
Gave credit to my eyes or ears,
But held the views an empty dream,
On Berkely's immaterial fcheme;
And pond'ring fad with troubled breaft
At length my rifing doubts exprefs'd.
"Ah, whither, thus by rebels fmitten,
Is fled th' omnipotence of Britain,
Or fail'd its ufual guard to keep,
Gone traunting or fall'n afleep *;

　* "Cry aloud: for he is god; either he is talking, or he is purfuing, or he is in a journey, or paradventure he fleepeth. —And they cried aloud, and cut themfelves after their manner with knives and lancets." 1 *Kings*, chap. xviii. The other original fubjects alluded to in the fubfequent part of this fpeech, may be found by the curious reader in the various and immortal works mentioned by the poet in the text. *Edit.*

As

As Baal his prophets left confounded,
And bawling vot'ries gafh'd and wounded?
Did not, retir'd to bow'rs Elyfian,
Great Mars leave with her his commiffion,
And Neptune erft, in treaty free,
Give up dominion o'er the fea?
Elfe where's the faith of fam'd orations,
Addrefs, debate, and proclamations,
Or courtly fermon, laureat ode,
And ballads on the wat'ry God;
With whofe high ftrains great George enriches
His eloquence of gracious fpeeches?
Not faithful to our Highland eyes,
Thefe deadly forms of vifion rife;
But fure fome Whig-infpiring fprite
Now palms delufion on our fight.
I'd fcarcely truft a tale fo vain,
Should revelation prompt the ftrain,
Or Offian's ghoft the fcenes rehearfe,
In all the melody of * Erfe."

    " Too long, quoth Malcolm, with confufion,
You've dwelt already in delufion,
As Sceptics, of all fools the chief,
Hold faith in creeds of unbelief.
I come to draw thy veil afide
Of error, prejudice, and pride.

    * Erfe, the ancient Scottifh language, in which Offian
wrote his poems.

    I                                    Fools

Fools love deception, but the wife
Prefer fad truths to pleafing lies.
For know, thofe hopes can ne'er fucceed
That truft on Britain's breaking reed.
For weak'ning long from bad to worfe,
By fatal atrophy of purfe,
She feels at length with trembling heart,
Her foes have found her mortal part.
As fam'd Achilles, dipt by Thetis
In Styx, as fung in antient ditties,
Grew all cafe-harden'd o'er like fteel,
Invulnerable, fave his heel,
And laugh'd at fwords and fpears, as fquibs,
And all difeafes, but the kibes;
Yet met at laft his fatal wound,
By Paris' arrow nail'd to th' ground:
So Britain's boafted ftrength deferts,
In thefe her empire's utmoft fkirts,
Remov'd beyond her fierce impreffions,
And atmofphere of omniprefence;
Nor to thefe fhores remoter ends,
Her dwarf omnipotence extends:
Whence in this turn of things fo ftrange,
'Tis time our principles to change.
For vain that boafted faith, which gathers
No perquifite, but tar and feathers,
No pay, but Whig's infulting malice,
And no promotion, but the gallows.

                    P                          I've

I've long enough ftood firm and fteady,
Half-hang'd for loyalty already :
And could I fave my neck and pelf,
I'd turn a flaming Whig myfelf,
And quit this caufe, and courfe, and calling,
Like rats that fly from houfe that's falling.
But fince, obnoxious here to Fate,
This faving wifdom comes too late,
Our nobleft hopes already croft,
Our fal'ries gone, our titles loft,
Doom'd to worfe fuff'rings from the mob.
Than Satan's furg'ries ufed on Job ;
What more remains but now with fleight,
What's left of us to fave by flight ?
   " Now raife thine eyes ; for vifions true
Again afcending wait thy view."
I look'd ; and clad in early light,
The fpires of Bofton rofe to fight ;
The morn o'er eaftern hills afar,
Illum'd the varying fcenes of war.
Great Howe had long fince in the lap
Of Loring taken out his nap,
And with the fun's afcending ray,
The cuckold came to take his pay.
When all th' encircling hills around,
With inftantaneous breaft-works crown'd,
With pointed thunders met his fight,
By magic rear'd the former night.

                                    Each

Each fummit, far as eye commands,
Shone peopled with rebellious bands.
Aloft their tow'ring heroes rife,
As Titans erft affail'd the fkies,
Leagu'd with fuperior force to prove,
The fcepter'd hand of Britifh Jove.
Mounds, pil'd on hills, afcended fair
With batt'ries plac'd in middle air,
That, rais'd like angry clouds on high,
Seem'd like th' artill'ry of the fky,
And hurl'd their fiery bolts amain,
In thunder on the trembling plain.
I faw along the proftrate ftrand,
Our baffl'd Gen'rals quit the land,
And, fwift as frighted mermaids, flee,
T' our boafted element, the fea!
Refign that long contefted fhore,
Again the prize of rebel-power,
And tow'rd their town of refuge fly,
Like convict Jews, condemn'd to die.
    Then tow'rd the north, I turn'd my eyes,
Where Saratoga's heights arife,
And faw our chofen vet'ran band,
Defcend in terror o'er the land;
T' oppofe this fury of alarms,
Saw all New-England wake to arms,
And ev'ry Yanky, full of mettle,
Swarm forth, like bees at found of kettle.

Not

Not Rome, when Tarquin rap'd Lucretia,
Saw wilder muft'ring of militia.
Thro' all the woods and plains of fight,
What mortal battles fill'd my fight,
While Britifh corfes ftrew'd the fhore,
And Hudfon ting'd his ftreams with gore!
What tongue can tell the difmal day,
Or paint the party-colour'd fray;
When yeomen left their fields afar,
To plow the crimfon plains of war;
When zeal to fwords transform'd their fhares,
And turn'd their pruning-hooks to fpears,
Chang'd tailor's geefe to guns and ball,
And ftretch'd to pikes the cobler's awl;
While hunters fierce, like mighty Nimrod,
Made on our troops a daring inroad;
And lev'lling fquint on barrel round,
Brought our beau-officers to ground;
While rifle-frocks fent Gen'rals cap'ring,
And redcoats fhrunk from leathern apron,
And epaulette and gorget run
From whinyard brown and rufty gun:
While fun-burnt wigs in high command,
Rufh furious on our frighted band,
And ancient beards and hoary hair,
Like meteors ftream in troubled air.
With locks unfhorne not Samfon more
Made ufelefs all the fhow of war,

                                        Nor

Nor fought with affes jaw for rarity,
With more fuccefs or fingularity.
I faw our vet'ran thoufands yield
And pile their mufkets on the field,
And peafant guards, in rueful plight,
March off our captur'd bands from fight;
While ev'ry rebel-fife in play,
To Yanky-doodle tun'd its lay,
And like the mufic of the fpheres,
Mellifluous footh'd their vanquifh'd ears.

   " Alas, faid I, what baleful ftar,
Sheds fatal influence on the war,
And who that chofen Chief of fame,
That heads this grand parade of fhame?"

   " There fee how Fate, great Malcolm cried,
Strikes with its bolts the tow'rs of pride.
Behold that martial Macaroni,
Compound of Phœbus and Bellona,
With warlike fword and fing-fong lay,
Equipp'd alike for feaft or fray,
Where equal wit and valour join;
This, this is he, the fam'd Burgoyne:
Who pawn'd his honour and commiffion,
To coax the Patriots to fubmiffion,
By fongs and balls fecure obedience,
And dance the ladies to allegiance.
Oft his camp mufes he'll parade,
At Bofton in the grand blockade,

                        And

And well invok'd with punch of arrack,
Hold converfe fweet in tent or barrack,
Infpir'd in more heroic fafhion,
Both by his theme and fituation ;
While Farce and Proclamation grand,
Rife fair beneath his plaftic hand.
For genius fwells more ftrong and clear
When clofe confin'd, like bottl'd beer :
So Prior's wit gain'd greater pow'r,
By infpiration of the tow'r ;
And Raleigh, faft in prifon hurl'd,
Wrote all the Hift'ry of the World :
So Wilkes grew, while in goal he lay,
More patriotic ev'ry day,
But found his zeal, when not confin'd,
Soon fink below the freezing point,
And public fpirit, once fo fair,
Evaporate in open air.
But thou, great favorite of Venus,
By no fuch luck fhalt cramp thy genius ;
Thy friendly ftars till wars fhall ceafe,
Shall ward th' ill fortune of releafe,
And hold thee faft in bonds not feeble,
In good condition ftill to fcribble.
Such merit Fate fhall fhield from firing,
Bomb, carcafe, langridge, and cold iron,
Nor trufts thy doubly laurell'd head,
To rude affaults of flying lead.

                 Hence

Hence in this Saratogue retreat,
For pure good fortune thou'lt be beat;
Not taken oft, releas'd or refcu'd,
Pafs for fmall change, like fimple Prefcott *;
But captur'd there, as Fates befall,
Shall ftand thy hand for't, once for all.
Then raife thy daring thoughts fublime,
And dip thy conqu'ring pen in rhyme,
And changing war for puns and jokes,
Write new Blockades and Maids of Oaks †."
   This faid, he turn'd, and faw the tale
Had dy'd my trembling cheeks with pale;

* General Prefcott was taken and exchanged feveral times
during the war.                                      *Edit.*

† 'The Maid of the Oaks and the Blockade of Bofton, are
farces—the firft acknowledged by General Burgoyne, the
other generally afcribed to him.

   The Editors cannot avoid congratulating the public on
the great advantage rendered to this, his mother-country, by
that rebel General Gates.   By fending us the illuftrious Bur-
goyne under fuch a capitulation, as to confine him here *in good
condition ftill to fcribble,* during the remainder of the war, he
procured to the theatre of our capital, an amufement which
leaves us no occafion to envy the happinefs of the Boftonians
during the fiege; as the *Heirefs* is thought by the beft critics
to be at leaft equal to the *Maid of Oaks.*   This is an additional
proof of the prophetic fpirit of Malcolm, who clearly forefaw
that fuch a work would be the produce of this timely capture.
                                                    *Edit.*

Then

Then, pitying, in a milder vein
Purfu'd the vifionary ftrain.

" Too much, perhaps, hath pain'd your views
Of vict'ries gain'd by rebel crews;
Now fee the deeds, not fmall nor fcanty,
Of Britifh Valour and Human'ty;
And learn from this aufpicious fight,
How England's fons and friends can fight,
In what dread fcenes their courage grows,
And how they conquer all their foes."

I look'd and faw in wintry fkies
Our fpacious prifon-walls arife,
Where Britons all their captives taming,
Plied them with fcourging, cold, and famine;
Reduc'd to life's concluding ftages,
By noxious food and plagues contagious.
Aloft the mighty * Loring ftood,
And thriv'd, like † Vampyre, on their blood;

And

---

* Loring was a Refugee from Bofton, made commiffary of
prifoners by General Howe. The confummate cruelties prac-
tifed on the American prifoners under Loring's adminiftra-
tion almoft exceed the ordinary powers of human invention.
If a fimple ftatement of facts relative to this bufinefs were
properly drawn up and authenticated, it would furnifh the
friends of humanity with new images of horror in contemplating
the ravages of war; efpecially a war that obtains the name of
Rebellion, and is carried on at a diftance from the eye of the
nation. The conduct of the Turks in putting all prifoners to

And counting all his gains arifing,
Dealt daily rations out of poifon.
Amid the dead that croud the fcene,
The moving fkeletons were feen.
At hand our troops in vaunting ftrains,
Infulted all their wants and pains,
And turn'd on all the dying tribe,
The bitter taunt and fcornful gibe :
And Britifh officers of might,
Triumphant at the joyful fight,
O'er foes difarm'd with courage daring,
Exhaufted all their tropes of fwearing.
Around all ftain'd with rebel blood,
Like Milton's lazar-houfe it ftood,
Where grim Defpair attended nurfe,
And Death was Gov'rnor of the houfe.
Amaz'd, I cried, " Is this the way,
That Britifh Valour wins the day ?"

death is certainly much more rational and humane, than that
of the Britifh army for the three firft years of the American
war, or till after the capture of Burgoyne. We except from
this general obfervation, the conduct of Lord Dorcefter in
Canada ; he acted on the common principles of war, as now
practifed in Europe.                                    *Edit.*

† The notion of Vampyres is a fuperftition, that has greatly
prevailed in many parts of Europe. They pretend it is a
dead body, which rifes out of its grave in the night, and
fucks the blood of the living.

Q                                    More

More had I faid, in ftrains unwelcome,
Till interrupted thus by Malcolm :
" Blame not, quoth he, but learn the reafon
Of this new mode of conqu'ring treafon.
'Tis but a wife, politic plan,
To root out all the rebel-clan ;
(For furely treafon ne'er can thrive,
Where not a foul is left alive :)
A fcheme, all other chiefs to furpafs,
And do th' effectual work to purpofe.
For war itfelf is nothing further,
But th' art and myftery of murther,
And who moft methods has effay'd,
Is the beft Gen'ral of the trade,
And ftands Death's Plenipotentiary,
To conquer, poifon, ftarve, and bury.
This Howe well knew, and thus began,
(Defpifing Carleton's coaxing plan,
Who kept his pris'ners well and merry,
And dealt them food like Commiffary,
And by paroles and ranfoms vain,
Difmifs'd them all to fight again :)
Whence his firft captives, with great fpirit,
He tied up for his troops to fire * at,

* This was done openly and without cenfure by the troops
under Howe's command in many inftances, on his firft con-
queft of Long-Ifland.

And

And hop'd they'd learn, on foes thus taken,
To aim at rebels without fhaking.
Then, wife in ftratagem, he plann'd
The fure deftruction of the land,
Turn'd famine, ficknefs, and defpair,
To ufeful enginry of war,
Inftead of cannon, mufket, mortar,
Us'd peftilence, and death, and torture,
Sent forth the fmall-pox, and the greater,
To thin the land of ev'ry traitor,
And order'd out with like endeavour,
Detachments of the prifon-fever ;
Spread defolation o'er their head,
And plagues in Providence's ftead,
Perform'd with equal fkill and beauty,
Th' avenging angel's tour of duty,
Brought all the elements to join,
And ftars t' affift the great defign ;
As once in league with Kifhon's brook,
Fam'd Ifrael's foes they fought and took.
Then proud to raife a glorious name,
And em'lous of his country's fame,
He bade thefe prifon-walls arife,
Like temple tow'ring to the fkies,
Where Britifh Clemency renown'd,
Might fix her feat on facred ground ;
(That Virtue, as each herald faith,
Of whole blood kin to Punic Faith ;)

Q 2                                Where

Where all her God-like pow'rs unveiling,
She finds a grateful fhrine to dwell in.
Then, at this altar for her honour,
Chofe this High-prieft to wait upon her,
Who with juft rites, in ancient guifes,
Prefents thefe human facrifices;
Great Loring, fam'd above all laymen,
A proper Prieft for Lybian Ammon,
Who, while Howe's gift his brows adorns,
Had match'd that deity in horns.
Here ev'ry day her vot'ries tell
She more devours than th' idol Bel;
And thirfts more rav'noufly for gore,
Than any worfhipp'd Power before.
That ancient Heathen Godhead, Moloch,
Oft ftay'd his ftomach with a bullock,
Or if his morning rage you'd check firft,
One child fuffic'd him for a breakfaft.
But Britifh Clemency, with zeal,
Devours her hundreds at a meal;
Right well by Nat'ralifts defined,
A Being of carniv'rous kind:
So erft * Gargantua pleas'd his palate,
And eat his pilgrims up for fallad.
Not bleft with maw lefs ceremonious,
The wide-mouth'd whale that fwallow'd Jonas;

* See Rabelais's Hiftory of the Giant Gargantua.

Like

Like earthquake gapes, to death devote,
That open fepulchre, her throat;
The grave, or barren womb you'd ftuff,
And fooner bring to cry, enough;
Or fatten up to fair condition,
The lean-flefh'd kine of Pharaoh's vifion.
  " Behold her temple where it ftands
Erect by fam'd Britannic hands;
'Tis the Black-hole of Indian ftructure,
New-built with Englifh architecture,
On plan, 'tis faid, contriv'd and wrote,
By Clive, before he cut his throat;
Who ere he took himfelf in hand,
Was her High-prieft in Nabob-land:
And when with conqu'ring glory crown'd,
He'd well enflav'd the nation round,
With pitying heart the gen'rous chief,
(Since flav'ry's worfe than lofs of life,)
Bade defolation circle far,
And famine end the work of war;
Thus loos'd their chains, and for their merits,
Difmifs them free to worlds of fpirits;
Whence they with gratitude and praife,
Return'd * t' attend his latter days,

---

* Clive in the latter years of his life conceived himfelf
perpetually haunted by the ghofts of thofe, who were the
victims of his Britifh humanity in the Eaft-Indies.

And

And hov'ring round his reftlefs bed,
Spread nightly vifions o'er his head.

"Now turn, he cried, to nobler fights,
And mark the prowefs of our fights :
Behold, like whelps of Britifh Lion,
The warriors, Clinton, Vaughan, and Tryon,
March forth with patriotic joy,
To ravifh, plunder, burn, deftroy.
Great Gen'rals, foremoft in the nation,
The journeymen of Defolation !
Like Samfon's foxes each affails,
Let loofe with firebrands in their tails,
And fpreads deftruction more forlorn,
Than they did in Philiftine corn.
And fee in flames their triumphs rife,
Illuming all the nether fkies,
And ftreaming, like a new Aurora,
The weftern hemifphere with glory !
What towns, in afhes laid, confefs
Thefe heroes' prowefs and fuccefs !
What blacken'd walls, or burning fane,
For trophies fpread the ruin'd plain !
What females, caught in evil hour,
By force fubmit to Britifh power,
Or plunder'd Negroes in difafter
Confefs King George their lord and mafter !
What crimfon corfes ftrew their way
Till fmoaking carnage dims the day !

                                    Along

Along the fhore, for fure reduction,
They wield their befom of deftruction.
Great Homer likens, in his Ilias,
To dog-ftar bright the fierce Achilles;
But ne'er beheld in red proceffion,
Three dog-ftars rife in conftellation;
Or faw in glooms of ev'ning mifty,
Such figns of fiery triplicity,
Which far beyond the comet's tail,
Portend deftruction where they fail.
Oh ! had Great-Britain's god-like fhore,
Produc'd but ten fuch heroes more,
They'd fpar'd the pains, and held the
Of this world's final conflagration,
Which, when its time comes, at a ftand,
Would find its work all done t' its hand !
    " Yet tho' gay hopes our eyes may blefs;
Indignant fate forbids fuccefs;
Like morning dreams our conqueft flies,
Difpers'd before the dawn arife."
    Here Malcolm paus'd; when, pond'ring long,
Grief thus gave utt'rance to my tongue.
" Where fhrink in fear our friends difmay'd,
And all the Tories' promis'd aid?
Can none amid thefe fierce alarms
Affift the pow'r of royal arms ?"
" In vain, he cried, our king depends,
On promis'd aid of Tory-friends,

I	When

When our own efforts want fuccefs,
Friends ever fail as fears increafe.
As leaves, in blooming verdure wove,
In warmth of fummer cloath the grove,
But when autumnal frofts arife,
Leave bare their trunks to wintry fkies;
So while your pow'r can aid their ends,
You ne'er can need ten thoufand friends,
But, once in want by foes difmay'd,
May advertife them ftol'n or ftray'd.
Thus, ere Great-Britain's ftrength grew flack,
She gain'd that aid, fhe did not lack,
But now in dread, imploring pity,
All hear unmov'd her dol'rous ditty;
Allegiance wand'ring turns aftray,
And faith grows dim for lack of pay.
In vain fhe tries by new inventions,
Fear, falfhood, flatt'ry, threats, and penfions,
Or fends Commifs'ners with credentials *
Of promifes and penitentials.

As

* The paffage that here follows is to be explained thus:
In the year 1778, after the war had been raging three years,
and we had heard of the capture of Burgoyne's army, our
good government concluded to give up all the objects for
which the conteft had been begun. It accordingly paffed an
act repealing all the acts of which the Americans complained,
provided they would refcind their declaration of Independence,
and continue to be our colonies. The Miniftry then fent over
three

As, for his fare o'er Styx of old,
The Trojan ftole the bough of gold,
And, left grim Cerb'rus fhould make head,
Stuff'd both his fobs with * gingerbread ;
Behold at Britain's utmoft fhifts,
Comes Johnftone, loaded with like gifts,
To venture thro' the Whiggifh tribe,
To cuddle, wheedle, coax, and bribe,
Enter their lands, and on his journey,
Pofleflion take, as King's Attorney,
Buy all the vaffals to protect him,
And bribe the tenants not t' eject him ;
And call, to aid his defp'rate miffion,
His petticoated politician,
While Venus, join'd t' affift the farce,
Strolls forth ambaffador for Mars.

three Commiffioners, Mr. Johnftone, Mr. Eden, and a certain
Lord, whofe name the Editors have forgot. Thefe commiffioners
(whether in imitation of Eneas, as the Poet fuppofes, or whe-
ther in purfuance of the great fyftem of Sir Robert Wal-
pole, as a politician would fuppofe, we cannot tell ; the con-
jectures of every one are apt to run in the channel of his own
trade,) began their operations, and finifhed them, by attempt-
ing to bribe individuals among the members of the States,
and of the army. This bait appears to have caught nobody
but Arnold. The *petticoated politician*, here mentioned,
is a woman of Philadelphia, through whofe agency they are
faid to have offered a bribe to Jofeph Read, Governor of
Pennfylvania.                                        *Edit.*

*  ———— Medicatam frugibus offam. Æneid. lib. vi. 410.

In vain he strives, (for while he lingers,
These mastiffs bite his off'ring fingers,)
Nor buys for George and realms infernal,
One spaniel, but the mongrel Arnold.
'Twere vain to paint in vision'd show,
The mighty nothings done by Howe;
What towns he takes in mortal fray,
As stations, whence to run away;
What conquests gain'd in battles warm,
To us no aid, to them no harm;
For still th' event alike is fatal,
Whate'er success attend the battle,
If he gain victory, or lose it,
Who ne'er had skill enough to use it;
And better 'twere, at their expence,
T' have drubb'd him into common sense,
And wak'd by bastings on his rear,
Th' activity, tho' but of fear.
By slow advance his arms prevail,
Like emblematic march of snail;
That, be Millennium nigh or far,
'Twould long before him end the war.
From York to Philadelphian ground,
He sweeps the mighty flourish round,
Wheel'd circ'lar by excentric stars,
Like racing boys at Prison-bars *,

Who

---

* *Prison-bars* is a kind of juvenile contest sufficiently de-
scribed here. How far our author is justifiable in comparing

to

Who take the adverfe crew in whole,
By running round the opp'fite goal;
Works wide the traverfe of his courfe,
Like fhip in ftorms' oppofing force,
Like mill-horfe, circling in his race,
Advances not a fingle pace,
And leaves no trophies of reduction,
Save that of canker-worms, deftruction.
Thus, having long both countries curft,
He quits them, as he found them firft,
Steers home difgrac'd, of little worth,
To join Burgoyne, and rail at North.
    " Now raife thine eyes, and view with pleafure,
The triumphs of his fam'd fucceffor."
I look'd, and now by magic lore,
Faint rofe to view the Jerfey fhore;
But dimly feen, in glooms array'd,
For Night had pour'd her fable fhade,
And ev'ry ftar, with glimm'rings pale,
Was muffled deep in ev'ning veil:
Scarce vifible in dufky night,
Advancing Red-coats * rofe to fight;

to it the operations of General Howe in America, we leave
to be determined by thofe military men who know the hiftory
of his manœuvres.                                    *Edit.*

* *Red-coats*, a term for Britifh-troops.        *Edit.*

The lengthen'd train, in gleaming rows,
Stole filent from their flumb'ring foes,
Slow mov'd the baggage, and the train,
Like fnails, crept noifelefs o'er the plain;
No trembling foldier dar'd to fpeak,
And not a wheel prefum'd to creak.
My looks my new furprize confefs'd,
Till by great Malcolm thus addrefs'd:
" Spend not thy wits in vain refearches;
'Tis one of Clinton's moon-light marches.
From Philadelphia now retreating,
To fave his anxious troops a beating,
With hafty ftride he flies in vain,
His rear attack'd on Monmouth plain:
With various chance the mortal fray
Is lengthen'd to the clofe of day,
When his tir'd bands, o'ermatch'd in fight,
Are refcu'd by defcending night;
He forms his camp with vain parade,
Till ev'ning fpreads the world with fhade,
Then ftill, like fome endanger'd fpark,
Steals off on tiptoe in the dark;
Yet writes his king, in boafling tone,
How grand he march'd by light of moon *.

                           I fee

---

* The circumftance of Gen. Clinton's official difpatches,
giving an account of his marching from Monmouth by moon-
light, furnifhed a fubject of fome pleafantry in America;
                                where

I fee him, but thou can'ft not; proud
He leads in front the trembling crowd,
And wifely knows, if danger's near,
'Twill fall the heavieft on his rear.
Go on, great Gen'ral, nor regard
The fcoffs of ev'ry fcribbling Bard,
Who fing how Gods that fatal night
Aided bv miracles your flight,
As once they us'd, in Homer's day,
To help weak heroes run away;
Tell how the hours at awful trial,
Went back, as erft on Ahaz' dial,
While Britifh Jofhua ftay'd the moon,
On Monmouth plains, for Ajalon:
Heed not their fneers and gibes fo arch,
Becaufe fhe fet before your march.
A fmall miftake, your meaning right,
You take her influence for her light;
Her influence, which fhall be your guide,
And o'er your Gen'ralfhip prefide.
Hence ftill fhall teem your empty fkull,
With vict'ries when the moon's at full,
Which by tranfition yet more ftrange,
Wane to defeats before the change;
Hence all your movements, all your notions,
Shall fteer by like excentric motions,

where it was known that the moon had fet two hours before
the march began.                                    *Edit.*

Eclips'd

Eclips'd in many a fatal crifis,
And dimm'd when Wafhington arifes.

 And fee how Fate, herfelf turn'd traitor,
Inverts the ancient courfe of nature,
And changes manners, tempers, climes,
To fuit the genius of the times.
See Bourbon forms his gen'rous plan,
Firft guardian of the rights of man,
And prompt in firm alliance joins,
To aid the Rebels proud defigns.
Behold from realms of eaftern day,
His fails innum'rous fhape their way,
In warlike line the billows fweep,
And roll the thunders of the deep.
See, low in equinoctial fkies,
The Weftern Iflands fall their prize.
See Britifh flags, o'ermatch'd in might,
Put all their faith in inftant flight,
Or broken fquadrons from th' affray,
Drag flow their wounded hulks away.
Behold his chiefs in daring fets,
D'Eftaings, De Graffes, and Fayettes,
Spread thro' our camps their dread alarms,
And fwell the fears of rebel-arms.
Yet, ere our empire fink in night,
One gleam of hope fhall ftrike the fight ;
As lamps that fail of oil and fire,
Collect one glimm'ring to expire.

       And

And lo where fouthern fhores extend,
Behold our union'd hofts defcend,
Where Charleftown views, with varying beams,
Her turrets gild th' encircling ftreams.
There by fuperior might compell'd,
Behold their gallant Lincoln yield *,
Nor aught the wreaths avail him now,
Pluck'd from Burgoyne's imperious brow.
See, furious from the vanquifh'd ftrand,
Cornwallis leads his mighty band !
The fouthern realms and Georgian fhore
Submit, and own the victor's pow'r.
Lo, funk before his wafting way,
The Carolinas fall his prey !
In vain embattl'd hofts of foes
Effay in warring ftrife t' oppofe.
See, fhrinking from his conqu'ring eye,
The rebel legions fall or fly ;
And, with'ring in thefe torrid fkies,
The northern laurel fades and dies †.

---

* General Lincoln was fecond in command in the army of General Gates, during the campaign of 1777, which ended in the capture of General Burgoyne. He is an officer of great reputation. He afterwards commanded the army in South-Carolina, and was taken prifoner with the garrifon of Charlef-town in 1780.     *Edit.*

† This refers to the fortune of General Gates, who after having conquered General Burgoyne in the North, was defeat-ed by Lord Cornwallis in the South.     *Edit.*

With

With rapid force he leads his band
To fair Virginia's fated ftrand,
Triumphant eyes the travell'd zone,
And boafts the fouthern realms his own.
Nor yet this hero's glories bright
Blaze only in the fields of fight ;
Not Howe's human'ty more deferving,
In gifts of hanging, and of ftarving ;
Not Arnold plunders more tobacco,
Or fteals more Negroes for Jamaica * ;
Scarce Rodney's felf, among th' Euftatians,
Infults fo well the laws of nations ;
Ev'n Tryon's fame grows dim, and mourning,
He yields the laurel crown of burning.
I fee with rapture and furprize,
New triumphs fparkling in thine eyes ;
But view, where now renew'd in might,
Again the rebels dare the fight."
　　I look'd, and far in fouthern fkies,
Saw Greene, their fecond hope, arife,
And with his fmall but gallant band,
Invade the Carolinian land.

* Arnold, in the year 1781, having been converted to our caufe, commanded a detachment of our army in Virginia; where he plundered many cargoes of negroes and of tobacco, and fent them to Jamaica for his own account. How far the Lords Rodney and Cornwallis might have excelled him in this kind of heroic atchievements, time will perhaps never difcover.　　　　　　　　　　　　　　　　*Edit.*

A 3

As winds in ſtormy circles whirl'd
Ruſh billowing o'er the darken'd world,
And, where their waſting fury roves,
Succeſſive ſweep th' aſtoniſh'd groves.
Thus where he pours the rapid fight,
Our boaſted conqueſts ſink in night,
And wide o'er all th' extended field,
Our forts reſign, our armies yield,
Till, now regain'd the vanquiſh'd land,
He lifts his ſtandard on the ſtrand.

  Again to fair Virginia's coaſt,
I turn'd and view'd the Britiſh hoſt,
Where Cheſapeak's wide waters lave
Her ſhores, and join th' Atlantic wave.
There fam'd Cornwallis tow'ring roſe,
And ſcorn'd ſecure his diſtant foes ;
His bands the haughty rampart raiſe,
And bid the royal ſtandard blaze.
When lo, where ocean's bounds extend,
I ſaw the Gallic ſails aſcend,
With fav'ring breezes ſtem their way,
And croud with ſhips the ſpacious bay.
Lo, Waſhington, from northern ſhores,
O'er many a region, wheels his force,
And Rochambeau, with legions bright,
Deſcends in terrors to the fight.
Not ſwifter cleaves his rapid way,
The eagle cow'ring o'er his prey,

            S                              Or

Or knights in fam'd romance that fly
On fairy pinions thro' the fky.
Amaz'd the Briton's ftartl'd pride,
Sees ruin wake on ev'ry fide ;
And, all his troops to fate confign'd,
By inftantaneous ftroke Burgoyn'd *.
Not Cadmus view'd with more furpri ,
From earth embattl'd armies rife,
When, by fuperior pow'r impell'd,
He fow'd with dragon's teeth the field.
Here Gallic troops in terror ftand,
There ruſh in arms the Rebel band ;
Nor hope remains from mortal fight,
Or that laft Britiſh refuge, flight.
I faw, with looks downcaft and grave,
The Chief emerging from his † cave,

---

* As great revolutions give birth to new ideas, and enlarge
the fcope of human knowledge, fo likewife they enrich lan-
guage by the addition of new words. From the French word
*lanterne*, which fignifies a lamp-poft, and from the circum-
ftance of fome men being hanged on fuch a poft in Paris during
the revolution, the language of that country is enriched with
a new verb ; a circumftance well known at Saratoga, has
likewife given a new verb to our own : *lanterner*, in French
(fpeaking of a man) fignifies to hang him, —— *to Burgoyne*,
in Engliſh, (fpeaking of an army) fignifies to take them all
prifoners. *Vive la Revolution !*       *Edit.*

† Alluding to the well-known fact of Cornwallis's taking up
his refidence in a cave, during the fiege of York-Town.

                                   (Where

(Where, chac'd like hare in mighty round,
His hunters earth'd him firft in ground,)
And, doom'd by Fate to rebel fway,
Yield all his captur'd hofts a prey.

There, while I view'd the vanquifh'd town,
Thus with a figh my friend went on:
" Beholdft thou not that band forlorn,
Like flaves in Roman triumphs borne;
Their faces length'ning with their fears,
And cheeks diftain'd with ftreams of tears,
Like *dramatis perfonæ* fage,
Equipt to act on Tyburn's ftage.
Lo thefe are they, who, lur'd by follies,
Left all and follow'd great Cornwallis;
True to their King, with firm devotion,
For confcience fake and hop'd promotion,
Expectant of the promis'd glories,
And new Millennial ftate of Tories.
Alas! in vain, all doubts forgetting,
They tried th' omnipotence of Britain;
But found her arm, once ftrong and brave,
So fhorten'd now fhe cannot fave.
Not more aghaft departed fouls,
Who rifk'd their fate on Popifh bulls,
And find St. Peter at the wicket
Refufe to counterfign their ticket,
When driv'n to purgatory back,
With all their pardons in their pack:

Than

Then Tories muft'ring at their ftations
On faith of royal proclamations.
As Pagan Chiefs at ev'ry crifis,
Confirm'd their leagues by facrifices,
And herds of beafts to all their deities,
Oblations fell at clofe of treaties :
Cornwallis thus, in ancient fafhion,
Concludes his league of cap'tulation,
And victims, due to Rebel-glories,
Gives this fin-off'ring up of Tories.
See where, reliev'd from fad embargo,
Steer off confign'd a recreant cargo,
Like old fcape-goats to roam in pain,
Mark'd like their great fore-runner, Cain.
The reft, now doom'd by Britifh leagues,
To juftice of refentful Whigs,
Hold worthlefs lives on tenure ill,
Of tenancy at Rebel-will,
While hov'ring o'er their forfeit perfons,
The gallows waits his fure reverfions.
  " Thou too, M'Fingal, ere that day,
Shalt tafte the terrors of th' affray.
See o'er thee hangs in angry fkies,
Where Whiggifh conftellations rife,
And while plebeian figns afcend,
Their mob-infpiring afpects bend,

That baleful Star, whofe * horrid hair
Shakes forth the plagues of down and tar !
I fee the pole, that rears on high
Its flag terrific thro' the fky ;
The Mob beneath prepar'd t' attack,
And tar predeftin'd for thy back !
Ah ! quit, my friend, this dang'rous home,
Nor wait the darker fcenes to come ;
For know that Fate's aufpicious door,
Once fhut to flight, is op'd no more,
Nor wears its hinge by various ftations,
Like Mercy's door in proclamations †.

  " But left thou paufe, or doubt to fly,
To ftranger vifions turn thine eye :
Each cloud that dimm'd thy mental ray,
And all the mortal mifts decay ;

* ———— From his horrid hair
Shakes peftilence and war.

                              MILTON.


† *The door of mercy is now open,* and *the door of mercy will be
fhut,* were phrafes fo often ufed in the proclamations of Britifh
Generals in America, that our timorous Poet feems to fear
that the hinge of that door will be worn out.   A general col-
lection of thefe proclamations, or an abridgement of them com-
prifed in a few volumes, would form a curious fyftem of rhetori-
cal tactics ; which might be of great utility to the French emi-
grant princes, and to thofe potentates of Europe, who are
going to fubdue the fpirit of Liberty in France.        *Edit.*

See

See more than human Pow'rs befriend,
And lo, their hostile forms ascend!
See tow'ring o'er th' extended strand,
The Genius of the western land,
In vengeance arm'd, his sword assumes,
And stands, like Tories, drest in plumes.
See o'er yon Council seat with pride,
How Freedom spreads her banners wide!
There Patriotism with torch addres'd,
To fire with zeal each daring breast!
While all the Virtues in their band,
Escape from yon unfriendly land,
Desert their ancient British station,
Possest with rage of emigration.
Honour, his business at a stand,
For fear of starving quits the land;
And Justice, long disgraced at Court, had
By Mansfield's sentence been transported.
Vict'ry and Fame attend their way,
Tho' Britain wish their longer stay,
Care not what George or North would be at,
Nor heed their writs of *ne exeat;*
But, fir'd with love of colonizing,
Quit the fall'n empire for the rising."
    I look'd, and saw, with horror smitten,
These hostile pow'rs averse to Britain.
When lo, an awful spectre rose,
With languid paleness on his brows;

                                    Wan

Wan dropfies fwell'd his form beneath,
And ic'd his bloated cheeks with death ;
His tatter'd robe expofed him bare,
To ev'ry blaft of ruder air ;
On two weak crutches propt he ftood,
That bent at ev'ry ftep he trod,
Gilt titles grac'd their fides fo flender,
One, " Regulation," t'other, " Tender ;"
His breaft-plate grav'd with various dates,
" The faith of all th' United States :"
Before him went his fun'ral pall,
His grave ftood dug to wait his fall.
I ftarted, and aghaft I cry'd,
" What means this fpectre at their fide ?
What danger from a Pow'r fo vain,
And why he joins that fplendid train ?"
" Alas, great Malcolm cry'd, experience
Might teach you not to truft appearance.
Here ftands, as dreft by fierce Bellona,
The ghoft of Continental Money *,

Of

* The defcription here given of the Continental paper-
money is not more remarkable as a fplendid example of the
fublime burlefque, than as a faithful picture of that financical
operation. The hiftory of this meafure has not been well
underftood in Europe ; it has, therefore, been generally con-
demned by thofe theorifts who have had occafion to refer to
it. They condemn it as having been *unneceffary* in its origin,
and *unequal* in its operation. The former opinion, doubtlefs,
arifes

Of dame Neceffity defcended,
With whom Credulity engender'd.

arifes from a total ignorance of the circumftances under which
the meafure was adopted; to the latter opinion I would op-
pofe one obfervation.

It is the nature of war, not only to be unjuft on the offen-
five, but to be *unequal* in its effects among individuals on
the defenfive. Some muft be killed, wounded, worn out
with fatigue, or plundered, and fubjected to burthens, for
which they are never indemnified; while others are enriched.
The bufinefs of money in a war is, as far as poffible, to equal-
lize its evils, and atone for the ravages of violence. This can
never be done to perfection by any money-fyftem that can be
imagined. All that can be faid, therefore, againft the paper
currency of America is, that it performed its work in a lefs
perfect manner, than a full Treafury of gold and filver would
have done; and even this affertion might be queftioned.

Though this money was counterfeited by waggon loads in
the Britifh garrifons, and fent into circulation in the country,
yet none of the confequences followed which were expected
from this manœuvre. The paper-money carried on the war for
five years; when it was called in at a great difcount, gave
place to other meafures which the circumftances of the country
rendered practicable, and went peaceably to reft, as here de-
fcribed by the Author.

The "weak crutches," called *Regulation* and *Tender*, on
which this *Spectre* is fupported, allude to the different acts of
the State-Legiflatures, made with the defign of maintaining
the credit of the Continental Paper. Some of thefe acts re-
gulated the prices of commodities, others made this paper a
legal tender in payment.                                   *Edit.*

5                                                       'Tho'

Tho' born with conftitution frail,
And feeble ftrength that foon muft fail ;
Yet ftrangely vers'd in magic lore,
And gifted with transforming pow'r,
His fkill the wealth Peruvian joins
With diamonds of Brazilian mines.
As erft Jove fell by fubtle wiles
On Danae's apron thro' the tiles,
In fhow'rs of gold : his potent hand
Shall fhed like fhow'rs thro' all the land. ‑
Lefs great the magic art was reckon'd,
Of tallies caft by Charles the Second,
Or Law's famed Miffifippi fchemes,
Or all the wealth of South-fea dreams.
For he of all the world alone
Owns the long-fought Philos'pher's Stone,
Reftores the fab'lous times to view,
And proves the tale of Midas true.
O'er heaps of rags he waves his wand,
All turn to gold at his command,
Provide for prefent wants and future,
Raife armies, victual, clothe, accoutre,
Adjourn our conquefts by effoign,
Check Howe's advance, and take Burgoyne,
Then makes all days of payment vain,
And turns all back to rags again.
In vain great Howe fhall play his part,
To ape and counterfeit his art ;

T                                In

In vain fhall Clinton, more belated,
A conj'rer turn to imitate it;
With like ill luck and pow'r as narrow,
They'll fare, like for'cers of old Pharaoh,
Who tho' the art they underftood
Of turning rivers into blood,
And caus'd their frogs and fnakes t'exift,
That with fome merit croak'd and hifs'd,
Yet ne'er, by ev'ry quaint device,
Could frame the true Mofaic lice.
He for the Whigs his arts fhall try,
Their firft, and long their fole ally;
A patriot firm, while breath he draws,
He'll perifh in his country's caufe;
And when his magic labours ceafe,
Lie bury'd in eternal peace.

   " Now view the fcenes in future hours,
That wait the fam'd European Pow'rs.
See where yon chalky clifs arife,
The hills of Britain ftrike your eyes:
Its fmall extenfion long fupply'd
By vaft immenfity of pride;
So fmall, that had it found a ftation
In this new world at firft creation,
Or were by Juftice doom'd to fuffer,
And for its crimes tranfported over,

We'd find full room for't in Lake Erie, or
That larger water-pond, Superior *,
Where North, on margin taking ſtand,
Would not be able to ſpy land.
No more, elate with pow'r, at eaſe
She deals her inſults round the ſeas ;
See, dwindling from her height amain,
What piles of ruin ſpread the plain ;
With mould'ring hulks her ports are fill'd,
And brambles clothe the cultur'd field !
See on her cliffs her Genius lies,
His hankerchief at both his eyes,

* This ſuppoſition, ſo far as it reſpeᴄts *Lake Superior*, is
not exaggerated. That Lake is 2200 miles in circumfer-
ence. The Editors find it their duty to vindicate the Poet
from a charge of a breach of delicacy, to which ſome ſuppoſe
this paſſage renders him liable. By ſaying, North " would
not be able to ſpy land," they imagine he means to ridicule
the misfortune of that noble Lord in the loſs of his ſight.
But we will teſtify to all his readers both preſent and future
(or at leaſt, to all *our* readers, as long as theſe our annotations
ſhall accompany this immortal work) that this Poem was
written and publiſhed, word for word as in this edition, ſeveral
years before the above misfortune happened to his lordſhip.
Therefore the Author muſt be pronounced innocent of the
leaſt deſign upon any thing more than mental blindneſs.
There is no alluſion to any other eyes in his lordſhip, than the
eyes of his underſtanding, which were ſuppoſed, by ſome peo-
ple at that time, to be wonderouſly dim ; eſpecially when con-
ſidered as belonging to the Argus of a great nation. *Edit.*

With

With many a deep-drawn figh and groan,
To mourn her ruin and his own!
While joyous Holland, France, and Spain,
With conqu'ring navies rule the main,
And Ruffian banners, wide unfurl'd,
Spread commerce round the eaftern world.
And fee (fight hateful and tormenting)
Th' Amer'can empire, proud and vaunting,
From anarchy fhall change her crafis,
And fix her pow'r on firmer bafis ;
To glory, wealth, and fame afcend,
Her commerce rife, her realms extend ;
Where now the panther guards his den,
Her defert forefts fwarm with men,
Her cities, tow'rs, and columns rife,
And dazzling temples meet the fkies ;
Her pines defcending to the main,
In triumph fpread the wat'ry plain ;
Ride inland lakes with fav'ring gales,
And croud her ports with whit'ning fails ;
Till to the fkirts of weftern day,
The peopl'd regions own her fway."
　　Thus far M'Fingal told his tale,
When thund'ring fhouts his ears affail,
And ftrait a Tory that ftood fentry,
Aghaft, rufh'd headlong down the entry,
And with wild outcry, like magician,
Difpers'd the refidue of vifion :

　　　　　　　　　　　　For

For now the Whigs intell'gence found
Of Tories muft'ring under ground,
And with rude bangs and loud uproar,
'Gan thunder furious at the door.
The lights put out, each Tory calls
To cover him, on cellar walls,
Creeps in each box, or bin, or tub,
To hide his head from wrath of mob,
Or lurks, where cabbages in row
Adorn'd the fide with verdant fhow,
M'Fingal deem'd it vain to ftay,
And rifk his bones in fecond fray ;
But chofe a grand retreat from foes,
In lit'ral fenfe, beneath their nofe.
The window then, which none elfe knew,
He foftly open'd and crept thro',
And crawling flow in deadly fear,
By movements wife made good his rear.
Then, fcorning all the fame of martyr,
For Bofton took his fwift departure ;
Nor dar'd look back on fatal fpot,
More than the family of Lot.
Not North, in more diftrefs'd condition,
Out-voted firft by Oppofition :
Nor good King George when that dire phantom
Of Independence comes to haunt him,
Which hov'ring round by night and day,
Not all his conj'rers yet can lay.

His